JOURNAPRENEUR

JOURNAPRENEUR

Pioneering the Digital Age of Black Journalism

Doni Glover

Doni Glover

JOURNAPRENEUR
Pioneering the Digital Age of Black Journalism

By Emmy Nominated
Award-Winning Journalist
Founder of BMORENews.com
Doni Glover

Edited By
Richard D. Eliott

CONTENTS

PART	v
DEDICATION	ix
FOREWORD	xi
PREFACE	xiii
INTRODUCTION	xvii

1 | Chapter 1: The Digital Transformation of News   1

2 | Chapter 2: The Legacy and Evolution of the Black Press   7

3 | Chapter 3: Founding BMORENews.com   12

4 | Chapter 4: The Role of BMORENews.com in Modern Journalism   18

5 | Chapter 5: Community Engagement and Impact   23

6 | Chapter 6: Challenges and Opportunities in the Digital Age   29

CONTENTS

7 | Chapter 7: The Power of Partnerships and Strategic Alliances   35

8 | Chapter 8: Embracing Innovation and Future Trends   41

9 | Chapter 9: Navigating Challenges and Embracing Resilience   47

10 | Chapter 10: The Future of Black Journalism   54

11 | Chapter 11: Comparative Analysis   61

12 | Chapter 12: Reflections and Future Directions   66

13 | Chapter 13: Celebrating Milestones and Looking Forward   71

EPILOGUE   77
AFTERWORD   83
PHOTO INSERT   86
PHOTO GALLERY LISTING   95
REFERENCES   99
ABOUT THE AUTHOR   103

DEDICATION

This book is dedicated to my grandchildren: Amari, Satori, and Avani. *Make Pop pop proud!*

This book is also dedicated to the memory of a Black Press icon: Claude Albert Barnett (September 16, 1889 – August 2, 1967). Barnett was a prominent American journalist, publisher, entrepreneur, philanthropist, civic activist, and Pan-Africanist. He founded the Associated Negro Press (ANP), the first international news agency for Black newspapers, and was a vocal advocate against segregation in the military and blood supply. Barnett played a crucial role in documenting the Civil Rights Movement in the United States and the struggles for independence in Africa. Alongside Robert S. Abbott and John H. Johnson, Barnett was one of the most influential African-American media entrepreneurs of the 20th century, significantly advancing the role of the Black Press in journalism, advertising, public relations, and professionalism.

FOREWORD

In *JOURNAPRENEUR: Pioneering the Digital Age of Black Journalism*, *BMORENews.com's* founder, Doni Glover, has masterfully connected the dots factually and historically.

From the first print published newspapers, helmed by African American publishers John Russwurm and Frederick Douglass in the 19th century, to his modern day digital publication, Doni identifies the challenges of delivering relevant and timely news to the community while being Black.

In the two decades that Doni has published *BMORENews.com*, the publishing industry has undergone major changes, yet he has been resilient and not just survived, but thrived! *BMORENews.com* has stayed true to its mission to cover news and developments from an African American/Black perspective.

Doni's book adeptly addresses the rapid transformation in this millennium from print to digital, while simultaneously chronicling the social implications and impacts from slavery to reconstruction and through the civil rights movement.

Running and sustaining *BMORENews* involves a prescient and courageous approach to business and Doni has demonstrated his savvy. In *JournaPreneur*, Doni adroitly captures his entrepreneurial experiences and challenges over the last two decades as an African American, with facts and insights that are straightforward and candid. Maintaining an authentic link with the community while

FOREWORD

effectively addressing marketing, advertising, content delivery, distribution and the absolute need to master and leverage the dynamic social media landscape are areas of note that speak to the timeliness and instructional need for the information shared in this book.

As I am penning this foreword, I am less than 10 days from traveling to The Cannes Lions Awards Conference in France. The conference is the world's largest gathering of publishers, influencers, producers, advertisers, entertainers, creators, authors, athletes and marketers. Up until a few years ago, very few Blacks attended this event and we will still be underrepresented as notable and accomplished publishers and business persons like Doni will not be on hand. I am only sorry that this book will not be published for Cannes Lions 2024. Please trust that *JOURNAPRENEUR: Pioneering the Digital Age of Black Journalism* will be a major talking point in 2025! I highly recommend this book for all in business who look for genuine information and inspiration. It will meet and probably exceed expectations.

- Robert Ingram

PREFACE

For those who seek you for direction, know that you are a torchbearer now.
– Congressman Kweisi Mfume

The newspaper industry has experienced a sweeping transition with the advent of the digital revolution, moving from traditional print methods to a digital-first approach characterized by innovation and adaptability. Since 2002, *BMORENews.com* has stood at the forefront of this transformation. "Memoirs of *BMORENews.com*: Innovating Black Journalism in the Digital Era" delves into the critical issues surrounding the evolution of the Black Press in this post-digital era, highlighting *BMORENews.com's* role in reshaping the media landscape and influencing emerging Black journalists. One story at a time, *BMORENews.com* works diligently to establish itself as a cornerstone of the Black Press, driving conversations and nurturing a new generation of Black journapreneurs and digijournapreneurs. The reduction in traditional newsroom jobs has actually created new freelance opportunities, signaling a definitive shift towards digital, and created more space for adaptive Black papers to better cover local and community events.

This examination raises questions about the sustainability of Black legacy newspapers amidst competition from digital advertising giants like Google and Facebook and the future employment prospects for aspiring Black journalists. John Naisbitt's *"Megatrends*

PREFACE

2000" predicted changes driven by digital technology, envisioning a more interconnected global economy and a resurgence in cultural nationalism. The rise of social media has fundamentally reshaped society over the past quarter-century while the Black Press has continued to evolve alongside its mainstream counterparts, extending its reach across radio, television, and, most recently, the internet.

Newspapers have long been the bedrock of democracy, fostering the free exchange of ideas and empowering citizens to hold governments accountable. For African Americans, Black legacy newspapers play a crucial dual role: promoting democracy and ensuring that Black voices are heard in a society where colonialist and imperialist legacies have hindered Black progress. Without these newspapers, African Americans risk becoming "invisible," with their issues either intentionally ignored or overlooked.

Black legacy newspapers offer what Ralph Ellison described as a "light," providing an essential perspective and bridging the gaps left by mainstream media. They amplify the voices of 44.4 million African Americans, persistently reminding the world that Black lives matter despite ongoing attempts to silence these voices. Dr. Tyrone Taborn, founder of Career Communications Group, underscores the vital role of the Black Press in securing the full participation of Black people in society. To this end, he launched STEMCITYUSA.com, dedicating his life to closing the digital divide and liberating Black and brown people from digital apartheid. Dr. Taborn has emerged as the foremost voice of Black news in the Metaverse, championing the cause of equity in the digital age.

Colonialist theories underpinning this discourse are countered by scholars like Ralph Ellison and Asa Hilliard, who offer alternative perspectives on the interaction between colonizers and the colonized. Hilliard argues that freedom, not slavery, has propelled Black people, both in America and abroad. Regardless of lineage, the collective Black experience in America has been characterized by pervasive racial hatred. Hilliard emphasizes the post-slavery mindset, focusing on freedom and self-sufficiency, even if it meant establishing one's own maroon colony. Understanding these differing viewpoints is crucial as we explore the realm of the Black Press. Scholars like Ellison and Hilliard aim to empower oppressed peoples to reclaim their humanity and attain full humanization, countering the dehumanizing effects of colonization. This restoration to full humanization underscores the Black Press's role, inherently understanding the imperative for oppressed individuals to reject objectification and strive for liberation. The enduring trauma from the colonization and enslavement of Africans across the Western hemisphere, as enunciated by Frantz Fanon, further highlights the indispensability of Black newspapers and their legacy.

John Brown Russwurm epitomized the unwavering advocate for Black people worldwide. As the founding junior editor of Freedom's Journal, Russwurm's life embodied Pan-Africanism at a time when the Black voice was indispensable. Recognizing the collective exploitation and colonization by European nations, Russwurm championed the establishment of a Black-owned newspaper to counteract control and racial animosity. The inaugural issue of Freedom's Journal on March 16, 1827, declared its mission: *"We wish to plead our own cause."* Russwurm and co-founder Samuel Cornish envisioned the newspaper as not just a news outlet but also an organizer, educator, and business advocate for Black communities nationwide.

The strategies employed by Black legacy newspapers, such as the Afro-American Newspaper in Baltimore, to thrive in the post-digital era are of particular interest. Given the dominance of digital advertising platforms, concerns loom over the employment prospects for emerging Black journalists as traditional newspaper roles decline.

PREFACE

Securing a substantial market share to sustain operations and retain talent presents a pressing challenge for Black legacy newspapers.

Reflecting on three decades as a journalist, I have witnessed the transformative journey that has shaped the contemporary journalism landscape. From traditional typesetting methods to the internet era and the ascent of social media, digital innovation has revolutionized news delivery. Today, digital news is ubiquitous, accessible through mobile devices, challenging all news outlets, including Black legacy newspapers, to adapt their strategies for success in this new era.

As a Black journalist, I acknowledge the indispensable role played by the Black Press in amplifying the voices of marginalized communities. Confronting systemic racism, Black legacy newspapers have been instrumental in spotlighting issues often sidelined by mainstream media. This research seeks to explain how these newspapers and other Black media have navigated the digital transition while upholding tradition and nurturing the next generation of Black journalists. What lies ahead for the Black Press, and how can it persist as a beacon of representation and advocacy in an ever-evolving media landscape? These are the driving questions underlying this inquiry into the state of Black journalism.

In the vast expanse of the digital realm, where information flows endlessly and connections form with a click, *BMORENews.com* stands as a beacon of resilience and innovation. From its humble origins to its current prominence, this digital platform has carved a unique path, shaping narratives, fostering community, and championing change. As we embark on a journey through the evolution of *BMORENews.com*, we uncover not just a website but a narrative of adaptation, empowerment, and growth. This book serves as a testament to the power of digital storytelling and the enduring impact of a platform driven by purpose, passion, and unwavering dedication to its community.

INTRODUCTION

In today's landscape, where false and misleading information proliferates across various media channels, the role of trusted sources such as the Black Press becomes increasingly crucial. As individuals grapple with an overwhelming influx of information, the tendency to rely on just a few trusted channels will intensify. In this context, narrowcasting emerges as a vital strategy for specialized media, enabling them to effectively reach micromarkets with precision. The Black Press, with its rich history and deep-rooted trust within its community, is uniquely positioned to thrive in this environment, promising a robust future in delivering reliable and impactful content. — **Dr. Tyrone Taborn, CCG**

Imagine a world without the Black Press. Since the founding of *Freedom's Journal* in 1827, Black newspapers have been a vital voice for African Americans, reflecting their experiences and advocating for their rights. This legacy, however, is now at a crossroads. The future of Black legacy newspapers is perilous, as digitization disrupts traditional media worldwide. This book explores how Black digital news outlets, particularly *BMORENews.com*, navigate these challenges while maintaining what I pray is an essential role in society.

The Black Press has a rich history that predates the United States' first Black newspaper. This legacy stretches beyond America; Sierra Leone pioneered Black-owned newspapers a quarter-century earlier in 1804, and Haiti followed suit in 1807, each amplifying the voices of the marginalized and countering racist and imperialist tropes in their respective nations.

The first Black newspaper in the world discovered in this study, *The Royal Gazette/The Sierra Leone Advertiser*, was published in 1804 in Freetown, Sierra Leone, by Abraham Hazeley, a British expatriate settler from Nova Scotia, whose father, Abraham Hazeley, Sr., was a Black Loyalist and freedman from Charleston, South Carolina, having fought for the British for his freedom (Fyfe, 1962). From 1817 to 1827, 457 issues were printed (Stanford, 2016).

Simultaneously, during the early nineteenth century, the leaders of the Haitian Revolution established their first newspapers as Haiti was divided into two states, with Henry Christophe in the north and Alexandre Pétion in the south and west operating competing printing presses (*Lagazetteroyale.com*).

Just over a decade later, in 1827, *Freedom's Journal*, the first Black newspaper in the United States, was founded in New York City by John Russwurm and Samuel Cornish, marking the inception of the enduring legacy of the Black Press in America. The founding of Freedom's Journal coincided with the abolition of slavery in New York, the first such instance in America. Its mission was clear: "We wish to plead our own cause."

By 1861, over 40 Black-owned newspapers circulated in the U.S., growing to 492 by 1921. Despite these numbers, advertising revenue has always been a challenge. An example of this systemic underinvestment is in a lawsuit filed by Black billionaire Byron Allen against powerhouse fast food chain McDonalds for spending a paltry $5 million of their $1.6 billion advertising budget in 2019 with Black-owned media outlets despite African-Americans representing 40% of McDonald's consumers.

Fast forward to today, and the number of Black newspapers in the U.S. has dwindled to under 200. The rise of digital news

INTRODUCTION

platforms has further strained these publications, forcing them to adapt or close their doors.

Digitization has transformed the newspaper industry, with newsrooms worldwide grappling with the shift from print to digital. Legacy newspapers face significant challenges, including declining print editions and workforce reductions. Black legacy newspapers, in particular, struggle to secure a market share against digital advertising giants like Google and Facebook.

This book examines how Black digital news outlets, such as *BMORENews.com*, sustain their viability and profitability in the evolving media landscape. It explores innovative revenue strategies, including crowdfunding, while also valuing traditional methods like strategic partnerships and corporate sponsorships. Additionally, it highlights the effectiveness of infomercials in maintaining engagement and generating profit. The goal is to identify sustainable approaches that keep subscribers engaged and ensure the financial health of these essential news platforms.

Reflecting on three decades as a journalist, I have witnessed the transformative journey of contemporary journalism. From traditional typesetting methods to the internet era and the ascent of social media, digital innovation has revolutionized news delivery. Today, digital news is ubiquitous, accessible through mobile devices, challenging all news outlets, including Black legacy newspapers, to adapt their strategies for success in this new era.

As a Black journalist, I recognize the indispensable role of the Black Press in amplifying marginalized voices. Confronting systemic racism, Black legacy newspapers have been instrumental in spotlighting issues often sidelined by mainstream media. This research seeks to explain how these newspapers and other Black media navigate the digital transition while upholding tradition and nurturing the next generation of Black journalists.

INTRODUCTION

What lies ahead for the Black Press? How can it persist as a beacon of representation and advocacy in an ever-evolving media landscape? These are the driving questions underlying this inquiry into the state of Black journalism. Through the lens of BMORENews.com, we will explore the future of the Black Press in the digital age, uncovering a narrative of resilience, innovation, and empowerment.

Chapter 1: The Digital Transformation of News

The Decline of Print Newspapers

The world of journalism has undergone a profound transformation over the past few decades. The advent of the internet and the rapid growth of digital technologies have fundamentally changed the way news is gathered, produced, distributed, shared, and consumed. Traditional print newspapers, once the dominant source of news for the public, have experienced a dramatic decline. This shift has been driven by a combination of technological advancements, changing consumer behaviors, and the rise of digital media platforms.

The decline of print newspapers can be traced back to the early 2000s when the internet began to gain widespread popularity and cell phone usage was also on the rise. Readers increasingly turned to online sources for news, attracted by the immediacy and convenience of digital content. The economic downturn of 2008 further exacerbated the decline, as advertising revenues plummeted and many newspapers struggled to stay afloat. Major metropolitan newspapers reduced their print editions, cut staff, and, in some cases, ceased operations entirely.

The impact of these changes has been significant. The reduction in print editions and staff cuts has led to a loss of experienced journalists and a decrease in the quality and depth of reporting. Smaller local newspapers have been hit particularly hard, resulting in news deserts where communities lack access to reliable local news. Additionally, the shift to digital has created challenges in monetizing online content, as consumers have become accustomed to free news and are often reluctant to pay for subscriptions. A new and dangerous threat to independent journalism is the rise of media consolidation, with companies such as Sinclair Media, Tribune Publishing and NewsCorp holding ownership of multiple newspapers and thereby limiting the perspectives available to inform and educate fellow citizens.

Despite these challenges, some print newspapers have managed to adapt and survive by embracing digital transformation. They have developed robust online platforms, diversified their revenue streams through digital subscriptions, and leveraged social media to engage with readers. These efforts highlight the resilience and adaptability of the journalism industry, even as it continues to navigate the complex landscape of the digital age.

The decline of print newspapers is not just a story of loss but also one of evolution. It underscores the need for innovation and adaptation in a rapidly changing world. As we look to the future, the lessons learned from this transition will be crucial in shaping the next era of journalism, ensuring that the vital role of the press in society endures.

The Rise of Digital News Platforms

As print newspapers faced declining circulation and advertising revenue, digital news platforms emerged as the new frontier for journalism. These platforms offered a range of advantages over traditional print media, including lower production costs, broader reach, and the ability to deliver news in real time. The proliferation of smartphones and mobile devices further accelerated the shift to digital, enabling readers to access news anytime, anywhere.

Digital news platforms have also democratized the production and distribution of news. Independent journalists, bloggers, and citizen reporters can now publish their work and reach a global audience without the need for a traditional newsroom. Social media platforms like TikTok, YouTube, LinkedIn, Twitter, Facebook, and Instagram have become essential tools for journalists, allowing them to engage with readers, share breaking news, and promote their work.

The Impact of Social Media on Journalism

Social media has had a profound impact on journalism, both as a distribution channel and as a source of news. Platforms like Twitter and Facebook have become critical for breaking news, with stories often unfolding in real time through tweets and posts. Journalists use social media to gather information, connect with sources, and gauge public opinion. However, the rise of social media has also introduced new challenges, including the spread of misinformation and the pressure to produce content quickly, sometimes at the expense of accuracy.

The viral nature of social media means that stories can gain widespread attention quickly, often leading to increased scrutiny and public discourse. This has empowered marginalized communities and grassroots movements, giving them a platform to amplify their voices and reach a broader audience. However, the same mechanisms that allow for rapid dissemination of information can also be exploited to spread false or misleading content, posing significant challenges for journalists and news consumers alike.

An additional factor that can, intentionally or otherwise, stifle the ability to use social media for journalism is censorship and selective rules that are more likely to be applied to Black journalists and journalists seeking to empower communities of color.

The Necessity for Black Digital News Outlets to Innovate

For Black legacy newspapers, the digital revolution presents both opportunities and challenges. These publications have historically played a crucial role in advocating for African American communities, providing a platform for voices often ignored by mainstream media. However, the transition to digital has not been easy. Many Black legacy newspapers face significant financial constraints and must compete with larger, well-funded digital platforms.

Innovation is essential for the survival and growth of Black digital news outlets. This includes adopting new technologies, exploring diverse revenue streams, and finding creative ways to engage with readers. For example, *BMORENews.com* has embraced digital tools to expand its reach and impact. Founded in 2002, *BMORENews.com* quickly recognized the potential of digital media to amplify Black voices and cover stories that matter to the African American community.

Embracing New Revenue Models

Traditional advertising models, which have long been the financial backbone of newspapers, are no longer sufficient in the digital age. While some major news outlets favor digital subscriptions, smaller outlets have to find other sources of revenue. Black digital news outlets must consider all models and be willing to explore new revenue models to ensure financial sustainability. Crowdfunding, for instance, allows readers to directly support journalism they value. Platforms like Patreon enable journalists to build a community of supporters who contribute financially in exchange for exclusive content and engagement.

Blockchain-based microtransactions represent another innovative revenue stream. By leveraging blockchain technology, digital news outlets can facilitate secure, small-scale payments for individual articles or content, allowing readers to pay only for what they consume. This model has the potential to generate revenue while maintaining accessibility and affordability for readers.

Additionally, hosting events and forming strategic partnerships can provide valuable revenue sources. Events such as conferences, workshops, and community gatherings not only generate income but also strengthen the relationship between the news outlet and its audience. Strategic partnerships with businesses, non-profits, and other media organizations can also create mutually beneficial opportunities for growth and sustainability. *BMORENews.com* has been able to build partnerships with a number of entities over the years.

Engaging and Retaining Subscribers

In the competitive digital landscape, engaging and retaining subscribers is paramount. Black digital news outlets must focus on building a loyal reader base by delivering high-quality, relevant content that is ideally providing a different perspective than traditionally provided. This involves understanding the needs and preferences of their audience and tailoring content accordingly. Personalized newsletters, targeted social media campaigns, and interactive multimedia content are effective ways to enhance reader engagement.

This commitment extends to going the extra mile for news stories. *BMORENews.com* reporters often cover stories that other news outlets overlook. They have a reputation for being the only news outlet, and often the only Black news outlet, present at many events. As a colleague from Pittsburgh put it, "*You have to run the ball over there where the other guy ain't!*" This dedication sets BMORENews.com apart and solidifies its place as a trusted source of news within the community.

Building a sense of community is also essential. Readers are more likely to remain loyal to a publication that values their input and fosters a sense of belonging. Creating spaces for reader interaction, such as comment sections, forums, and social media groups, encourages active participation and strengthens the bond between the publication and its audience.

Conclusion

The digital transformation of news presents both significant challenges and exciting opportunities for journalism, particularly for Black digital news outlets. The decline of print newspapers and the rise of digital platforms have reshaped the media landscape, necessitating innovation and adaptation. By embracing new revenue models, leveraging social media, and prioritizing reader engagement, Black digital news outlets can continue to play a vital role in advocating for African American communities and ensuring their voices are heard.

BMORENews.com stands as a testament to the potential of digital journalism to drive change and make a lasting impact. As we move forward in this digital age, the lessons learned from *BMORENews.com* and similar outlets will be invaluable in shaping the future of the Black Press and ensuring its continued relevance and success.

Chapter 2: The Legacy and Evolution of the Black Press

Historical Roots of the Black Press

The Black Press has long been a crucial voice for African Americans, dating back to the early 19th century. The first Black-owned and operated newspaper, *Freedom's Journal*, was established in 1827 by John Russwurm and Samuel Cornish in New York City. Its founding marked a pivotal moment in American journalism, providing a platform for African Americans to *"plead our own cause."* The paper covered issues relevant to the Black community, from abolitionist activities to social and economic injustices, filling a void left by mainstream media.

Prior to *Freedom's Journal*, the world saw its first Black-owned newspaper in Sierra Leone in 1804, *The Royal Gazette/The Sierra Leone Advertiser*. Published by Abraham Hazeley, a British expatriate settler, this publication underscored the global reach and importance of the Black Press in advocating for African diasporic communities. In 1807, Haiti followed with its own Black newspaper amidst the Haitian Revolution's success, further emphasizing the critical role of Black journalism in the fight for freedom and representation.

The Golden Age of the Black Press

By the mid-19th century, the Black Press in the United States had grown significantly. By 1861, there were over 40 Black-owned newspapers circulating, a number that continued to grow as the century progressed. These newspapers played an essential role during the Civil War and Reconstruction, advocating for the rights of freed Blacks and providing crucial information to the broader Black community.

The early 20th century marked the Golden Age of the Black Press. Publications like *The Chicago Defender*, founded in 1905, became influential in the Great Migration, encouraging African Americans to move north for better opportunities. *The Defender* and other Black newspapers were instrumental in challenging segregation, advocating for civil rights, and covering stories ignored by the mainstream press.

By the summer of 1921, the Negro Press in the United States revealed there were 492 Black newspapers. This proliferation underscored the demand for news tailored to the African American experience, addressing issues like Jim Crow laws, lynching, and economic disparity. These publications not only informed but also inspired and mobilized Black communities while creating jobs and promoting opportunities specifically for the Black community.

Challenges and Decline

Despite their crucial role, Black newspapers have faced persistent challenges, particularly in securing advertising revenue. Historically, mainstream businesses were reluctant to advertise in Black publications, limiting their financial resources and distribution. This challenge has persisted into the modern era, compounded by the digital disruption of the newspaper industry.

The decline of print newspapers in the late 20th and early 21st centuries has hit the Black Press hard. Many publications struggled to transition to digital platforms due to limited financial and technological resources. By 2023, the number of Black newspapers in the U.S. had dwindled to around 167, a stark contrast to their peak.

Adapting to the Digital Age

The rise of digital media has necessitated a significant shift for Black newspapers. While some have struggled, others have successfully adapted, leveraging the internet to expand their reach and continue their mission. Digital platforms offer opportunities for broader distribution, real-time news updates, and multimedia storytelling, which are crucial for engaging modern audiences.

Case Study: BMORENews.com

BMORENews.com exemplifies the successful transition of a Black news outlet to the digital age. Founded in 2002, *BMORENews.com* emerged during a time when the internet was still gaining traction as a primary news source. Recognizing the potential of digital media, DMGlobal positioned *BMORENews.com* as a pioneering force in Black digital journalism.

The Role of Social Media

Social media has become an indispensable tool for Black digital news outlets. Platforms like Twitter, Facebook, Instagram, and YouTube allow these outlets to engage with their audience, share stories in real time, and amplify voices that might otherwise go unheard. For *BMORENews.com*, social media has been a vital component of its strategy, enabling it to build a robust online community and expand its influence. The low costs and ease of targeting ads along with the presence of groups that often distribute information has made social media a particularly convenient place to receive news, although worries regarding racist censorship, poor moderation, and the prevalence of misinformation are often viewed as major criticisms of social media as a tool rather than problems that companies can attempt to fix.

The Importance of Community Engagement

A key strength of the Black Press has always been its deep connection to the community. Digital platforms have enhanced this engagement, allowing outlets to interact with their audience more directly and personally. *BMORENews.com* has leveraged this capability to host political forums, talent shows, and community meetings, ensuring that it remains a vital part of the community it serves.

Financial Sustainability in the Digital Era

Financial sustainability remains a critical challenge for Black digital news outlets. Traditional advertising revenue models are no longer sufficient, necessitating the exploration of alternative revenue streams. Crowdfunding, subscriptions, and partnerships with businesses and nonprofits are some of the strategies being employed to ensure financial viability.

BMORENews.com has embraced these strategies, utilizing crowdfunding and forming strategic partnerships to support its operations. Additionally, hosting events has become a significant revenue source, further solidifying its role as a community hub.

The Future of the Black Press

The future of the Black Press lies in its ability to adapt and innovate. Digital platforms offer immense potential for reaching wider audiences and engaging with communities in new and meaningful ways. However, this transition requires a commitment to quality journalism, ethical standards, and financial sustainability.

BMORENews.com stands as a testament to the resilience and adaptability of the Black Press. By leveraging digital tools and embracing new revenue models, it has continued to serve its community and uphold the legacy of Black journalism.

Conclusion

The legacy of the Black Press is one of resilience, advocacy, and empowerment. From its early days with *Freedom's Journal* to the digital innovations of *BMORENews.com*, Black newspapers have been crucial in amplifying African American voices and advocating for their rights. As the media landscape continues to evolve, the Black Press must continue to adapt, innovate, and remain steadfast in its mission to serve and empower the African American community.

In the face of digital disruption, the Black Press's commitment to its core values will ensure its continued relevance and impact. The journey of *BMORENews.com* highlights the potential of digital journalism to drive change and make a lasting difference, providing a blueprint for the future of the Black Press in the digital age.

3

Chapter 3: Founding BMORENews.com

The Genesis of BMORENews.com

BMORENews.com was born out of a vision to create a platform that would amplify the voices of African Americans and cover stories often overlooked by mainstream media. In 2002, during a period when the internet was rapidly evolving, I saw an opportunity to harness digital technology to serve the Black community in Baltimore and beyond. The early 2000s were marked by the dominance of AOL ("You have mail!"), the rise of MySpace, and a burgeoning interest in digital media. This was the perfect environment for a new, innovative news outlet to take root.

Early Challenges and Breakthroughs

The initial years of *BMORENews.com* were characterized by both challenges and breakthroughs. Establishing a digital news outlet at a time when the internet was still considered a novelty required a leap of faith. It also meant educating people. Traditional newspapers were still the primary source of news for most people, and the concept of an online-only news platform was relatively uncharted territory. In retrospect, a part of the tasks involved introducing people to the internet. One of the first stories published was one on Donald Edward Glover (my dad). While he did not have access to the internet at the time, he went to the public library, pulled up the story, and printed it out. This was around 2003 and showed me first-hand that people would indeed go to the website – if they had a reason.

Securing funding and resources was one of the significant challenges. Unlike established newspapers with decades of history and infrastructure, *BMORENews.com* had to build its reputation and audience from scratch. This meant navigating financial constraints, technological hurdles, and the skepticism of potential supporters who were more familiar with print media.

Despite these obstacles, *BMORENews.com* persevered. Like my dad said, *"If you get out there and try, somebody might see you and even help you. But you will never know if you never try"*. Another saying goes like this: **"You miss 100% of the shots you do not take."** Our determination and vision attracted a dedicated team of contributors who shared the commitment to covering stories that mattered to the Black community. The platform began to gain traction, drawing readers who appreciated its focus on local issues, Black entrepreneurship, and community empowerment.

Pioneering Digital Journalism

BMORENews.com quickly established itself as a trailblazer in digital journalism. By adopting digital tools and social media early on, the platform distinguished itself from traditional newspapers. Embracing these technologies enabled *BMORENews.com* to deliver news in real-time, engage directly with readers, and create multimedia content that resonated with a digital audience.

A significant part of *BMORENews.com's* success was its expertise in Maryland politics. Covering areas from Baltimore to the Eastern Shore, Western Maryland, and the DC suburbs, this small news outlet has always maintained strong political contacts throughout the state. Over the years, *BMORENews.com* has featured important stories, particularly focusing on minority business enterprise (MBE) and the development of Maryland's Black political power.

One of the platform's critical innovations was its use of video content. *BMORENews.com* recognized the power of video to tell compelling stories and connect with viewers on a deeper level. It built one of the largest Black news video libraries, featuring thousands of videos covering a wide range of topics. This extensive video content became a cornerstone of *BMORENews.com's* strategy, attracting a broad audience and establishing the platform as a leader in digital storytelling.

Building a Community-Centric Platform

From its inception, *BMORENews.com* has been deeply connected to the community it serves. The platform's coverage of local events, political forums, and community meetings has fostered a strong sense of connection with its audience. This community-centric approach is a core aspect of *BMORENews.com's* identity, ensuring it remains relevant and responsive to the needs of its readers.

A prime example of this commitment is the Joe Mann's Black Wall Street Awards, an initiative by *BMORENews.com*. These awards honor Black entrepreneurs, professionals, and allies across various U.S. cities, celebrating their contributions and promoting economic empowerment within the Black community. By recognizing these individuals, *BMORENews.com* not only highlights their achievements but also inspires others to pursue their entrepreneurial dreams. Since 2011, *BMORENews.com* has honored over 2,700 individuals in nine major U.S. cities, reflecting its dedication to community engagement and empowerment.

Strategic Partnerships and Collaborations

Strategic partnerships have played a crucial role in the growth and sustainability of *BMORENews.com*. Collaborating with businesses, nonprofits, and other media organizations has provided valuable resources and expanded the platform's reach. These partnerships have enabled *BMORENews.com* to offer more diverse content, host events, and engage with a broader audience.

One notable partnership is with Career Communications Group (CCG), led by Dr. Tyrone Taborn. This collaboration has been instrumental in elevating *BMORENews.com's* profile and providing access to a wealth of knowledge and expertise in digital media and journalism. CCG's support has helped *BMORENews.com* navigate the complexities of the digital landscape and explore new opportunities for growth. Better yet, our *"Doni Glover Show"* earned an Emmy-nomination in 2023 thanks to CCG. Other partnerships include the US Black Chambers, BWI-Thurgood Marshall Airport, the Bea Gaddy Family Center, The Men's Center, the Greater Baltimore Black Chamber of Commerce, the West North Avenue Development Authority, the Arce Fundacion, Chesapeake Habitat for Humanity, the Central Intercollegiate Athletic Association Basketball Tournament, James Mosher Baseball, and the Salvation Army of Central Maryland.

Financial Sustainability and Innovation

Financial sustainability has always been a central concern for *BMORENews.com*. Traditional advertising revenue models, while still important, are no longer sufficient to support a digital news outlet. *BMORENews.com* has explored various revenue streams, including crowdfunding, subscriptions, and hosting events. These strategies have provided the financial stability needed to continue its mission of serving the Black community.

One innovative approach has been the integration of blockchain-based microtransactions. This technology allows readers to make small payments for individual articles or content, offering a flexible and secure way to support the platform. By diversifying its revenue sources, *BMORENews.com* has ensured its financial viability while maintaining accessibility and affordability for its readers.

Adapting to the Digital Age

The digital age is characterized by rapid technological advancements and changing consumer behaviors. *BMORENews.com's* ability to adapt to these changes has been a key factor in its success. The platform continuously updates its digital tools, explores new content formats, and stays attuned to the preferences of its audience.

Social media remains a vital component of *BMORENews.com's* strategy. Platforms like Twitter, Facebook, Instagram, Tik Tok, and YouTube provide essential channels for distributing content, engaging with readers, and building a loyal community. *BMORENews.com's* proactive approach to social media ensures that it remains at the forefront of digital journalism, leveraging these platforms to amplify its voice and reach a wider audience.

Impact and Legacy

Over two decades, *BMORENews.com* has made a significant impact on the landscape of Black journalism. The platform has covered stories that might have otherwise been overlooked, provided a voice for the African American community, and championed issues of social justice and economic empowerment. Its innovative approach to digital journalism has set a precedent for other Black news outlets, demonstrating the potential of digital media to drive change and make a lasting difference.

BMORENews.com's legacy is one of resilience, innovation, and community engagement. As it continues to evolve, the platform remains committed to its mission of amplifying Black voices and covering stories that matter. The journey of *BMORENews.com* serves as an inspiration for future generations of journalists and media entrepreneurs, highlighting the power of digital technology to transform journalism and empower communities.

Conclusion

The founding of *BMORENews.com* marks a significant chapter in the history of Black journalism. From its humble beginnings to its current prominence, *BMORENews.com* has navigated the challenges of the digital age with determination and vision. By embracing innovation, fostering community engagement, and ensuring financial sustainability, *BMORENews.com* has carved out a unique space in the media landscape.

As we look to the future, *BMORENews.com's* journey offers valuable lessons for other Black digital news outlets. The platform's success underscores the importance of adaptability, innovation, and a deep connection to the community. In an ever-changing media environment, these principles will be crucial for ensuring the continued relevance and impact of the Black Press.

4

Chapter 4: The Role of BMORENews.com in Modern Journalism

Redefining Black Journalism in the Digital Era

BMORENews.com has played a transformative role in redefining Black journalism in the digital age. Its innovative approach has filled a critical gap in mainstream media and set new standards for delivering news to the African American community. By leveraging digital tools and platforms, *BMORENews.com* has expanded the reach of Black journalism, ensuring the stories and perspectives of African Americans are prominently featured in the digital narrative.

Amplifying Underrepresented Voices

BMORENews.com's commitment to amplifying underrepresented voices is one of its most significant contributions. Mainstream media often overlooks issues affecting the Black community or fails to provide comprehensive coverage. *BMORENews.com* addresses this disparity by focusing on stories that matter most to African Americans, from local community events and political developments to social justice issues and entrepreneurial success stories. Its extensive video library and robust social media presence ensure these voices are heard, capturing the nuances of the African American experience in ways traditional print media often cannot.

Community Engagement and Empowerment

BMORENews.com prioritizes community engagement and empowerment. The platform serves as a bridge between the news and the community, fostering a two-way dialogue that keeps readers informed and engaged. This approach builds trust and empowers the community by providing the information and resources needed to make informed decisions. The Joe Mann's Black Wall Street Awards exemplify this commitment by recognizing Black entrepreneurs and professionals, inspiring others to pursue their goals, and contributing to the economic development of their communities.

Navigating Financial Sustainability

Financial sustainability is a critical challenge for all media organizations, and *BMORENews.com* is no exception. However, the platform has demonstrated resilience and innovation in navigating this challenge. Traditional advertising revenue models have been supplemented with various other income streams, including crowdfunding, partnerships, and event hosting. *BMORENews.com* has explored innovative revenue models such as blockchain-based microtransactions, allowing readers to pay for individual pieces of content. This approach provides a steady revenue stream while maintaining accessibility. By diversifying its revenue sources, *BMORENews.com* has built a sustainable business model that supports its mission of serving the Black community.

Strategic Use of Social Media

Social media has been a game-changer for *BMORENews.com*, providing a powerful tool for distribution, engagement, and community building. The platform's active presence on Twitter, Facebook, Instagram, and YouTube has enabled it to reach a broader audience and engage with readers in real-time. *BMORENews.com's* strategic use of social media goes beyond mere distribution, creating meaningful interactions with its audience, responding to comments, and fostering a sense of community. Social media analytics provide valuable insights into audience preferences and behaviors, allowing *BMORENews.com* to tailor its content and engagement strategies effectively.

Highlighting Black Entrepreneurship

A significant focus of *BMORENews.com* is highlighting Black entrepreneurship. The platform regularly features stories of Black business owners and professionals, showcasing their achievements and the challenges they face. This coverage provides visibility for these individuals and promotes economic empowerment within the Black community. The Joe Mann's Black Wall Street Awards are a key initiative in this regard, celebrating the accomplishments of Black entrepreneurs across various U.S. cities. By honoring these individuals, *BMORENews.com* recognizes their contributions and inspires others to pursue entrepreneurial endeavors, fostering a culture of economic self-sufficiency and growth.

Advocating for Social Justice

BMORENews.com has been a steadfast advocate for social justice, using its platform to highlight issues such as police brutality, systemic racism, and economic inequality. The platform's in-depth coverage of social justice issues provides critical context and analysis, helping to inform and mobilize the community. Through its reporting, *BMORENews.com* has shed light on injustices and advocated for change. The platform's commitment to social justice is evident in its coverage of major events and movements, from the protests following the death of Freddie Gray in Baltimore to the Black Lives Matter movement. By giving a voice to the marginalized and holding those in power accountable, *BMORENews.com* fulfills its role as a watchdog for the community.

Educational Initiatives and Youth Engagement

Education is a pillar of *BMORENews.com's* mission. The platform has launched several initiatives aimed at educating and engaging the youth, including internships, mentorship programs, and partnerships with educational institutions. *BMORENews.com* provides opportunities for young aspiring journalists to gain hands-on experience and learn from industry professionals, equipping the next generation with the skills and knowledge they need to succeed. By investing in youth education and engagement, *BMORENews.com* ensures the continued growth and evolution of Black journalism.

The Future of BMORENews.com

As *BMORENews.com* looks to the future, it remains committed to its core mission of serving the African American community.

The platform will continue to innovate, leveraging new technologies and exploring new revenue models to ensure its sustainability. Social media will remain a key tool for engagement, allowing *BMORENews.com* to connect with its audience and amplify their voices. *BMORENews.com* will also continue to focus on community empowerment, social justice, and educational initiatives. By staying true to these values, the platform will not only maintain its relevance but also drive meaningful change in the community. The journey of *BMORENews.com* serves as a powerful example of how digital journalism can transform the media landscape and empower communities.

Conclusion

BMORENews.com has redefined Black journalism in the digital age, setting new standards for how news is delivered and consumed. Through its innovative approach, commitment to community engagement, and advocacy for social justice, *BMORENews.com* has made a lasting impact on the media landscape. The platform's success is a testament to the power of digital technology to drive change and make a difference. As *BMORENews.com* continues to evolve, it will undoubtedly remain a vital voice for the African American community, providing a blueprint for the future of Black journalism. The role of *BMORENews.com* in modern journalism is not just about reporting news; it's about empowering a community, advocating for justice, and inspiring future generations.

5

Chapter 5: Community Engagement and Impact

The Essence of Community Engagement

BMORENews.com has always understood the vital importance of community engagement. From its inception, the platform has aimed to be more than just a news outlet; it has aspired to be a bedrock of the community it serves. This chapter delves into the various ways *BMORENews.com* engages with its community and the profound impact of these efforts on both the platform and the community at large.

The Joe Manns Black Wall Street Awards

One of the flagship initiatives of *BMORENews.com* is the Joe Mann's Black Wall Street Awards. These awards celebrate Black entrepreneurs, professionals, and allies across the United States. Since its launch, the awards have recognized over 2,500 individuals in nine U.S. cities, including New York, Baltimore, Washington D.C., Richmond, Atlanta, New Orleans, Birmingham, Las Vegas, and Tulsa. The significance of these awards lies in their dual purpose: honoring those who have made substantial contributions to their communities and inspiring others to pursue entrepreneurial and professional excellence. The awards ceremonies are more than just celebratory events; they are platforms for networking, mentorship, and community building.

Political Forums and Community Meetings

BMORENews.com has hosted numerous political forums and community meetings, providing a platform for dialogue and civic engagement. These events have included debates, town hall meetings, and discussions on pressing local and national issues. By bringing together community members, politicians, and thought leaders, these forums foster a deeper understanding of the issues and promote active participation in the democratic process. These engagements have proven particularly effective in holding public officials accountable and ensuring that the voices of the African American community are heard in political discourse. *BMORENews.com's* commitment to these initiatives underscores its role as a catalyst for community involvement and advocacy.

Talent Shows and Cultural Events

BMORENews.com also plays a crucial role in promoting cultural enrichment through talent shows and other cultural events. These events provide a platform for local artists, musicians, and performers to showcase their talents and celebrate their cultural heritage. By highlighting the rich cultural diversity within the African American community, *BMORENews.com* helps to foster a sense of pride and unity. These events also serve as opportunities for community members to come together, share experiences, and strengthen social bonds. The emphasis on cultural engagement reflects *BMORENews.com's* broader mission of celebrating and preserving African American culture and identity.

Prison Ministry and Youth Outreach

Recognizing the importance of supporting the most vulnerable members of the community, *BMORENews.com* launched a prison ministry program focused on youths aged 14 to 17 charged with adult crimes in 2007. This program aims to provide mentorship, guidance, and support to these young individuals, helping them navigate the challenges of incarceration and reintegrate into society. In addition to its prison ministry, *BMORENews.com* is deeply committed to youth outreach. The platform collaborates with schools, colleges, and youth organizations to provide educational opportunities, internships, and mentorship programs. By investing in the youth, *BMORENews.com* ensures that the next generation is equipped with the skills, knowledge, and confidence to succeed.

Partnerships with Educational Institutions

BMORENews.com's partnerships with educational institutions are a testament to its commitment to education and professional development. The platform has established relationships with several schools, colleges, and universities, offering internships and practical training for aspiring journalists and media professionals. These partnerships provide students with hands-on experience in digital journalism, helping them develop critical skills and gain valuable insights into the industry. *BMORENews.com's* investment in education not only benefits the students but also enriches the platform with fresh perspectives and innovative ideas.

Collaborations with Nonprofits and Community Organizations

Collaborating with nonprofits and community organizations has been a cornerstone of *BMORENews.com's* community engagement strategy. These partnerships amplify the platform's impact by leveraging the resources, expertise, and networks of various organizations committed to social justice, economic empowerment, and community development. Through these collaborations, *BMORENews.com* has been able to support a wide range of initiatives, from affordable housing projects and healthcare access campaigns to voter registration drives and small business development programs. These efforts align with the platform's mission to address systemic inequities and promote the well-being of the African American community.

Impact on Local and National Discourse

BMORENews.com's community engagement efforts have had a significant impact on both local and national discourse. By providing a platform for underrepresented voices and addressing issues that are often neglected by mainstream media, *BMORENews.com* has influenced public opinion and policy on various fronts. The platform's in-depth coverage of local issues, coupled with its national reach, ensures that the concerns and achievements of the African American community receive the attention they deserve. This has been particularly evident in the coverage of social justice movements, political campaigns, and economic initiatives.

Building a Legacy of Trust and Credibility

At the heart of *BMORENews.com's* community engagement efforts is a commitment to building trust and credibility. The platform's consistent focus on transparency, accountability, and ethical journalism has earned it the trust of its readers and the broader community. By actively engaging with the community, *BMORENews.com* demonstrates its dedication to serving as a reliable source of information and a staunch advocate for social justice. This trust is a cornerstone of the platform's success and a critical factor in its continued relevance and impact.

The Road Ahead: Continuing the Mission

As *BMORENews.com* looks to the future, it remains steadfast in its mission to serve and uplift the African American community. The platform will continue to explore new ways to engage with its audience, leverage technology to enhance its impact, and build partnerships that further its goals. Community engagement will remain a central pillar of *BMORENews.com's* strategy, ensuring that it remains deeply connected to the people it serves. By continuing to listen to and learn from the community, *BMORENews.com* will be well-positioned to address emerging challenges and seize new opportunities.

Conclusion

BMORENews.com's commitment to community engagement and impact is evident in every aspect of its work. From celebrating Black excellence through the Joe Mann's Black Wall Street Awards to hosting political forums and supporting youth through educational initiatives, *BMORENews.com* has established itself as a vital force in the community. These efforts have not only strengthened the platform's connection to its audience but also made a tangible difference in the lives of countless individuals. As *BMORENews.com* continues to evolve, its dedication to community engagement will remain a driving force, guiding its mission and ensuring its lasting impact.

6

Chapter 6: Challenges and Opportunities in the Digital Age

Navigating the Digital Landscape

The digital revolution has transformed the media landscape, presenting both challenges and opportunities for journalism. For *BMORENews.com*, navigating this new terrain has required adaptability, innovation, and a steadfast commitment to its mission. This chapter explores the various challenges *BMORENews.com* has faced in the digital age and the strategies it has employed to turn these challenges into opportunities.

The Decline of Traditional Print Media

One of the most significant challenges in the digital age has been the decline of traditional print media. As readers increasingly turn to digital platforms for news, print newspapers have seen a dramatic drop in circulation and advertising revenue. This shift has forced many legacy newspapers to downsize or shut down entirely.

For *BMORENews.com*, being a digital-native platform has been an advantage. Unlike traditional print newspapers, *BMORENews.com* was built with the digital landscape in mind. This foresight has allowed the platform to avoid many of the pitfalls that have plagued print media. However, it also means constantly staying ahead of technological advancements and evolving reader preferences.

Financial Sustainability

Financial sustainability remains a critical challenge for digital news outlets. The traditional advertising revenue model has been disrupted by digital advertising giants like Google and Facebook, which command a significant share of the market. This has made it difficult for smaller news outlets to compete for advertising dollars.

BMORENews.com has addressed this challenge by diversifying its revenue streams. In addition to traditional advertising, the platform has explored crowdfunding, partnerships, and event hosting as alternative sources of income. For instance, the Joe Mann's Black Wall Street Awards not only celebrate Black excellence but also serve as revenue-generating events. By creating multiple income streams, *BMORENews.com* has built a more resilient financial foundation.

The Rise of Social Media

Social media has revolutionized how news is distributed and consumed. Platforms like Twitter, Facebook, Instagram, and YouTube have become essential tools for reaching audiences and driving engagement. However, they also present challenges, such as the spread of misinformation and the need to constantly adapt to changing algorithms.

BMORENews.com has leveraged social media to its advantage, using it to amplify underrepresented voices and engage with the community in real-time. The platform's active presence on social media has helped it build a loyal following and increase its reach. *BMORENews.com* also uses social media analytics to gain insights into audience preferences and tailor its content accordingly.

Maintaining Journalistic Integrity

In an age where clickbait and sensationalism often drive traffic, maintaining journalistic integrity is more important than ever. *BMORENews.com* has stayed true to its mission of providing accurate, fair, and comprehensive coverage of issues affecting the African American community. This commitment simultaneously includes elevating Black issues to the forefront of the discussion, countering misinformation and racist notions, and building community relationships to ensure unique perspectives into ongoing events.

The platform's commitment to ethical journalism has helped it build trust with its audience. By focusing on in-depth reporting and quality content, *BMORENews.com* has differentiated itself from less reputable sources and established itself as a reliable news outlet.

Technological Advancements

The rapid pace of technological advancements presents both challenges and opportunities for digital news outlets. Staying updated with the latest tools and technologies is crucial for maintaining a competitive edge. However, it also requires continuous investment in training and infrastructure.

BMORENews.com has embraced technological advancements to enhance its reporting and engagement efforts. The platform has invested in video production, livestreaming, and mobile-friendly design to ensure it meets the needs of its digital-savvy audience. Additionally, *BMORENews.com* is exploring emerging technologies like artificial intelligence and blockchain to further innovate its operations.

Engaging a Diverse Audience

Engaging a diverse audience in the digital age requires understanding and addressing the unique needs and preferences of different demographic groups. For *BMORENews.com*, this means creating content that resonates with the African American community while also appealing to a broader audience interested in issues of social justice and equity.

The platform has achieved this by producing a wide range of content, from news articles and opinion pieces to videos and podcasts. By offering diverse content formats and topics, *BMORENews.com* ensures that it reaches and engages a wide audience.

Collaboration and Partnerships

Collaboration and partnerships have been pivotal for *BMORENews.com* in navigating the digital landscape. By working with other news and information outlets, such as Kenny Brown's *Northwest Voice Newspaper* in Baltimore County, Wayne Frazier's Maryland Washington Minority Companies Association, Dr. Michael Carter's BlackWallStreet.org in Oakland, California, and Dr. Eric Kelly, III, founder of the Black Business Network (which includes Black Expo USA, the Black Business Olympics, and the Black Business Hall of Fame – hailed as "one of the largest Black business showcases in history") based in Durham, NC (an official Black Wall Street city), as well as community organizations like the Greater Baltimore Urban League and educational institutions like Morgan State University's School of Global Journalism and Communication, *BMORENews.com* has significantly expanded its reach and impact. These partnerships have enabled *BMORENews.com* to share resources, cross-promote content, and collaborate on special projects. For example, the platform's partnerships with educational institutions have provided valuable opportunities for student journalists to gain hands-on experience and contribute to *BMORENews.com's* mission.

Addressing Digital Divide

Despite the widespread use of digital technology, the digital divide remains a significant issue, particularly in underserved communities. Ensuring that all members of the community have access to digital news is a challenge that *BMORENews.com* is committed to addressing.

The platform has implemented initiatives to bridge the digital divide, such as providing digital literacy training and advocating for affordable internet access. By working to ensure that everyone has the tools and knowledge to access digital news, *BMORENews.com* is helping to create a more inclusive information ecosystem.

Future Directions

Looking ahead, *BMORENews.com* is focused on continuing to innovate and adapt to the ever-changing digital landscape. The platform will explore new technologies and revenue models to enhance its operations and ensure its sustainability.

BMORENews.com is also committed to deepening its community engagement efforts and expanding its reach. By staying true to its mission and values, the platform will continue to be a vital resource for the African American community and a leader in digital journalism.

Conclusion

The digital age has brought about profound changes in the media landscape, presenting both challenges and opportunities. *BMORENews.com's* ability to navigate these changes with innovation, resilience, and a commitment to its mission has been key to its success.

By embracing digital tools, diversifying revenue streams, maintaining journalistic integrity, and engaging with the community,

BMORENews.com has turned challenges into opportunities. As it continues to evolve, the platform will remain a vital force in digital journalism, ensuring that the stories and voices of the African American community are heard and valued.

7

Chapter 7: The Power of Partnerships and Strategic Alliances

Introduction

In the rapidly evolving landscape of digital media, partnerships and strategic alliances have become crucial for sustainability and growth. For *BMORENews.com*, these collaborations have not only extended its reach but also strengthened its impact within the community. This chapter explores the significance of these partnerships, the key alliances that have been formed, and how they have contributed to the platform's success.

The Role of Strategic Partnerships

Strategic partnerships enable media organizations to pool resources, share expertise, and leverage each other's strengths. For *BMORENews.com*, forming alliances with like-minded organizations has been a strategic move to enhance its capabilities and expand its influence.

These partnerships have provided *BMORENews.com* with access to new audiences, additional content, and innovative technologies.

By working together, partners can tackle challenges more effectively and achieve mutual goals, leading to a more robust and sustainable media ecosystem.

Key Partnerships and Collaborations

National Newspaper Publishers Association (NNPA)

Joining the National Newspaper Publishers Association (NNPA) is a goal for *BMORENews.com*. Founded in 1940, the NNPA serves as a trade association for nearly 200 African American-owned community newspapers across the United States. Members gain valuable insights and support from a network of established Black newspapers, enhancing its editorial standards and operational practices.

Black Media Initiative at CUNY's Newmark School of Journalism

BMORENews.com is, however, a part of the Black Media Initiative at the Craig Newmark Graduate School of Journalism at the City University of New York. Launched in 2020, this initiative supports Black media outlets through advocacy, events, training, and research. The director, Cheryl Thompson-Morton, is doing a magnificent job uplifting Black media across the country and is to be saluted.

BMORENews.com has benefited from the resources and training provided by the Black Media Initiative, which have helped the platform stay current with industry trends and best practices. This partnership also facilitates networking opportunities with other

Black media professionals, fostering a collaborative environment that drives innovation and growth.
LION (Local Independent Online News) Publishers
BMORENews.com is also a member of LION Publishers which is dedicated to fortifying the local news industry by empowering independent news publishers to build more sustainable businesses. Its primary focus is on the business side of news entrepreneurship, as many other organizations are already helping publishers enhance their journalism skills.

LION's mission is to support over 475 members across the U.S. and Canada in creating and managing successful news enterprises. These are businesses capable of paying a living wage, attracting and retaining talent, expanding their reach, revenue, and impact, and establishing a lasting presence in their communities.

Local Community Organizations

BMORENews.com has established partnerships with various local community organizations to amplify its impact on the ground. They include the Men's Center in Historic East Baltimore, Druid Heights Community Development Corporation, the East Baltimore Development, Inc., and the Sandtown Community Collective. Collaborations with nonprofits like Fusion Partnership, educational institutions, and grassroots organizations have enabled *BMORENews.com* to support a wide range of community initiatives, from affordable housing projects to voter registration drives.

These partnerships have been instrumental in promoting social justice and economic empowerment within the African American community. By working with local organizations, *BMORENews.com* ensures that its efforts are aligned with the community's needs and priorities.

DONI GLOVER

Collaborative Projects and Initiatives

The Joe Mann's Black Wall Street Awards

The Joe Mann's Black Wall Street Awards, a flagship initiative of *BMORENews.com*, exemplifies the power of collaboration. These awards recognize Black entrepreneurs, professionals, and their allies, celebrating their contributions to the community. The success of these events is largely due to partnerships with local businesses, sponsors, and community leaders.

These collaborations not only provide financial support but also enhance the credibility and reach of the awards. By working together, partners help create a platform that honors excellence and inspires future generations of Black professionals and entrepreneurs.

Political Forums and Community Engagement

BMORENews.com's political forums and community meetings are other examples of effective collaboration. These events bring together politicians, community leaders, and residents to discuss pressing issues and promote civic engagement.

Partnerships with educational institutions, civic organizations, and media outlets have been crucial in organizing and promoting these forums. By leveraging the resources and networks of its partners, *BMORENews.com* can facilitate meaningful dialogue and foster a more informed and engaged community.

Leveraging Technology through Partnerships

In the digital age, staying ahead of technological advancements is essential for media organizations. *BMORENews.com* has formed strategic alliances with technology partners to enhance its digital capabilities and improve user experience.

These partnerships have enabled *BMORENews.com* to invest in video production, livestreaming, and mobile-friendly design, ensuring that its content is accessible and engaging. Additionally, exploring emerging technologies like artificial intelligence and blockchain through these alliances positions *BMORENews.com* at the forefront of digital innovation.

Building a Network of Support

The power of partnerships extends beyond formal collaborations to include a network of mentors, advisors, and supporters. For *BMORENews.com*, this network has been instrumental in navigating challenges and seizing opportunities.

Key figures like Diane Bell McKoy, Michael Preston, Dr. Charles Simmons, Ricky Smith, and J. Howard Henderson have provided invaluable guidance and support. Their mentorship has helped shape *BMORENews.com's* strategic direction and operational practices, ensuring its long-term success.

Future Directions for Strategic Partnerships

Looking ahead, *BMORENews.com* will continue to prioritize strategic partnerships as a core component of its growth strategy. The platform aims to deepen existing collaborations and explore new alliances that align with its mission and values.

Future partnerships will focus on expanding *BMORENews.com's* reach, enhancing its technological capabilities, and driving social impact. By fostering a collaborative ecosystem, *BMORENews.com* can continue to be a leading voice in digital journalism and a champion for the African American community.

Conclusion

The power of partnerships and strategic alliances cannot be overstated. For *BMORENews.com*, these collaborations have been pivotal in navigating the challenges of the digital age and amplifying its impact. By working together with like-minded organizations like James Mosher Baseball and individuals like Dr. Wilbert Wilson, Sandy Pruitt, Joe Gaskins, Mark Spencer, and Ervin Reid in Prince George's County, *BMORENews.com* has built a resilient and dynamic platform that continues to serve and uplift the community.

As *BMORENews.com* moves forward, it will remain committed to leveraging the power of partnerships to drive innovation, foster growth, and make a lasting difference in the lives of its readers and the broader community.

8

Chapter 8: Embracing Innovation and Future Trends

The Importance of Innovation in Journalism

In an era where information is abundant and technology evolves at a rapid pace, innovation is critical for the survival and growth of media organizations. *BMORENews.com*, as a digital-native platform, has consistently embraced innovation to stay relevant and impactful. This chapter explores the innovative strategies and future trends that will shape the future of *BMORENews.com* and digital journalism as a whole.

Technological Advancements and Their Impact

The integration of new technologies has revolutionized how news is gathered, produced, and consumed. *BMORENews.com* has been at the forefront of adopting these advancements, ensuring that it delivers timely and engaging content to its audience.

Video Production and Livestreaming

Video content has become a dominant form of media consumption. Recognizing this trend, *BMORENews.com* has invested heavily in video production and livestreaming capabilities. This investment has enabled the platform to provide real-time coverage of events, interviews, and breaking news, offering viewers an immersive experience.

By utilizing platforms like YouTube, Facebook Live, and Instagram Live, *BMORENews.com* reaches a wider audience and engages viewers through interactive content. The emphasis on video not only enhances storytelling but also caters to the preferences of a digitally-savvy audience. Some of our video content has even gone viral.

Mobile-Friendly Design

With the majority of news consumers accessing content via mobile devices, ensuring a seamless mobile experience is paramount. *BMORENews.com* has prioritized mobile-friendly design, optimizing its website and content for mobile viewing. This approach has made it easier for users to access news on-the-go, increasing engagement and accessibility. Many thanks to the techies in our arsenal, including William Hopson, Alexis Coates, Jevon Spivey, and Andy Pierre.

The Role of Artificial Intelligence

Artificial Intelligence (AI) is transforming the media landscape, offering new ways to analyze data, personalize content, and automate processes. *BMORENews.com* is exploring AI applications to enhance its operations and deliver a more tailored experience to its audience.

Data Analytics and Personalization

AI-driven data analytics allow *BMORENews.com* to gain deeper insights into audience behavior and preferences. By analyzing user data, the platform can tailor content recommendations, ensuring that readers receive news that is relevant to their interests. This level of personalization enhances user engagement and satisfaction.

Automation and Efficiency

AI can automate repetitive tasks, freeing up journalists to focus on in-depth reporting and creative storytelling. For *BMORENews.com*, this means using AI tools for tasks such as transcription, content curation, and social media management. Automation increases efficiency and allows the platform to produce more content without compromising quality.

Blockchain and Digital Security

Blockchain technology offers innovative solutions for digital security, content verification, and monetization. *BMORENews.com* is exploring the potential of blockchain to address challenges related to digital rights management and content authenticity.

Protecting Intellectual Property

Blockchain can provide a secure and transparent way to manage digital rights and protect intellectual property. For *BMORENews.com*, this means safeguarding its content from unauthorized use and ensuring that creators are properly credited and compensated.

Enhancing Trust and Transparency

In an age where misinformation is rampant, maintaining trust and transparency is crucial. Blockchain technology can be used to verify the authenticity of news content, providing a transparent record of its creation and distribution. This enhances credibility and helps combat the spread of fake news.

Virtual and Augmented Reality

Virtual Reality (VR) and Augmented Reality (AR) are emerging technologies that offer new dimensions to storytelling. *BMORENews.com* is exploring the use of VR and AR to create immersive news experiences that engage and inform audiences in innovative ways.

Immersive Storytelling

VR and AR can transport viewers to the scene of a story, providing a first-person perspective that traditional media cannot offer. *BMORENews.com* aims to leverage these technologies to create immersive documentaries, interactive news reports, and virtual tours that bring stories to life.

Audience Engagement

AR can enhance audience engagement by overlaying digital information onto the real world. For *BMORENews.com*, this could mean creating interactive graphics, augmented reality advertisements, or educational content that enhances the user experience and fosters deeper engagement.

The Future of Social Media

Social media continues to be a vital tool for news distribution and audience engagement. As social media platforms evolve, *BMORENews.com* is committed to staying ahead of trends and leveraging these platforms to their fullest potential.

Building Online Communities

BMORENews.com recognizes the power of social media to build and nurture online communities. By actively engaging with followers on platforms like Facebook, Twitter, Instagram, and LinkedIn, the platform fosters a sense of community and encourages meaningful conversations around news topics.

Leveraging Emerging Platforms

Staying ahead in the digital age means being open to new and emerging social media platforms. *BMORENews.com* continuously evaluates new platforms to determine their potential for reaching and engaging new audiences. By being an early adopter, the platform can establish a strong presence and capitalize on new opportunities for growth.

Continuous Learning and Adaptation

The media landscape is in a constant state of flux, driven by technological advancements and changing consumer behaviors. For *BMORENews.com*, continuous learning and adaptation are essential to staying relevant and competitive.

Professional Development

Investing in the professional development of its team is a priority for *BMORENews.com*. The platform encourages its journalists and staff to stay updated with the latest industry trends, tools, and best practices. This commitment to learning ensures that the team remains skilled and innovative.

Feedback and Iteration

Listening to audience feedback and iterating based on insights is crucial for continuous improvement. *BMORENews.com* actively seeks feedback from its readers and uses it to refine its content, design, and user experience. This iterative approach helps the platform stay attuned to audience needs and preferences.

Conclusion

Innovation is the lifeblood of *BMORENews.com*, driving its mission to deliver high-quality, impactful journalism. By embracing new technologies, exploring emerging trends, and fostering a culture of continuous learning, *BMORENews.com* is well-positioned to navigate the challenges and opportunities of the digital age.

As the media landscape continues to evolve, *BMORENews.com* will remain committed to innovation, ensuring that it continues to serve as a vital resource for the African American community and a leader in digital journalism. The future is bright, and with a forward-thinking approach, *BMORENews.com* is poised to thrive in the ever-changing world of digital media.

Chapter 9: Navigating Challenges and Embracing Resilience

Introduction

The journey of *BMORENews.com*, like any entrepreneurial venture, has been filled with challenges and obstacles. However, it is through these trials that resilience and determination have been forged, driving the platform to greater heights. This chapter delves into the challenges faced by *BMORENews.com*, the strategies employed to overcome them, and the lessons learned along the way.

The Financial Landscape

One of the most significant challenges for any media organization, especially a digital news outlet, is financial sustainability. *BMORENews.com* has navigated various financial hurdles, from securing initial funding to maintaining steady revenue streams in a competitive market.

Securing Initial Funding

Starting *BMORENews.com* required a leap of faith and a keen understanding of resource management. The initial funding came from personal savings, small investments, and support from key individuals who believed in the vision. These early investments were crucial in building the foundation of the platform.

Diversifying Revenue Streams

To ensure financial stability, *BMORENews.com* diversified its revenue streams. Advertising has been a primary source of income, but the platform also explored other avenues such as sponsored content, events, and partnerships. Hosting events like the Joe Manns Black Wall Street Awards provided both revenue and community engagement opportunities.

The Role of Grants and Donations

Grants and donations from supporters and philanthropic organizations have played a significant role in sustaining *BMORENews.com*. By aligning with organizations that support the mission of promoting Black journalism and community empowerment, *BMORENews.com* has been able to secure funding that aligns with its values and goals.

Technological Challenges

The rapid pace of technological advancement presents both opportunities and challenges. Staying up-to-date with the latest tools and platforms is essential but can also be daunting.

Adapting to Digital Innovations

BMORENews.com has continuously adapted to technological changes by investing in digital innovations such as video production, livestreaming, and mobile-friendly design. Staying ahead of technological trends has allowed the platform to provide a high-quality user experience and maintain relevance in the digital age.

Cybersecurity

Ensuring the security of digital assets and user data is paramount. *BMORENews.com* has faced cybersecurity challenges, including hacking attempts and data breaches. Implementing robust security measures and protocols has been essential in protecting the integrity of the platform and the trust of its audience.

Content and Audience Engagement

Creating engaging and impactful content while maintaining journalistic integrity is a constant challenge. *BMORENews.com* has developed strategies to ensure high-quality content that resonates with its audience.

Maintaining Journalistic Integrity

Balancing the need for revenue with the commitment to unbiased reporting is crucial. *BMORENews.com* has adhered to strict editorial guidelines to ensure that content remains credible and trustworthy. This integrity has been a staple of the platform's reputation.

Engaging a Diverse Audience

BMORENews.com serves a diverse audience with varying interests and needs. Tailoring content to engage this wide range of readers requires a deep understanding of the community and continuous feedback. By leveraging data analytics and audience insights, *BMORENews.com* has been able to create content that resonates with its readers.

Competition and Market Dynamics

The media landscape is highly competitive, with numerous outlets vying for audience attention and advertising dollars. *BMORENews.com* has navigated this competition by differentiating itself and carving out a unique niche.

Differentiation and Branding

Building a strong brand identity has been key to standing out in a crowded market. *BMORENews.com* has positioned itself as a leading voice in Black journalism, emphasizing its commitment to community empowerment and social justice. This clear brand identity has attracted a loyal audience and distinguished the platform from competitors.

Strategic Alliances

Forming strategic alliances with other media organizations and community groups has provided *BMORENews.com* with a competitive edge. These partnerships have expanded its reach, enhanced content quality, and provided additional resources to tackle market challenges.

The Impact of Social and Political Climate

The social and political climate can significantly impact media organizations. *BMORENews.com* has navigated various socio-political challenges, from reporting on sensitive issues to advocating for social change.

Reporting on Sensitive Issues

Covering sensitive topics such as racial inequality, police brutality, and political corruption requires careful consideration and a commitment to ethical journalism. *BMORENews.com* has approached these issues with a focus on accuracy, empathy, and advocacy, providing a platform for marginalized voices.

Advocacy and Social Change

BMORENews.com has not only reported on social issues like the discrimination faced by the historically Black Hoe's Heights Community at the hands of some neighboring Roland Park community members but also actively participated in advocacy efforts. By partnering with community organizations and participating in social justice movements, the platform has contributed to meaningful change and demonstrated its commitment to the community.

Resilience and Lessons Learned

The journey of *BMORENews.com* is a testament to resilience and the ability to adapt and thrive despite challenges. Key lessons learned include the importance of flexibility, continuous learning, and maintaining a strong support network.

Flexibility and Adaptation

The ability to adapt to changing circumstances and pivot when necessary has been crucial for *BMORENews.com*. Whether it's embracing new technologies or adjusting business strategies, flexibility has enabled the platform to navigate challenges effectively.

Continuous Learning

Staying informed about industry trends, technological advancements, and audience preferences is essential for sustained success. *BMORENews.com* has prioritized continuous learning and professional development, ensuring that the team remains knowledgeable and innovative.

Building a Support Network

Having a strong support network of mentors, advisors, and partners has been invaluable. This network has provided guidance, resources, and encouragement, helping *BMORENews.com* navigate challenges and seize opportunities.

Conclusion

Navigating challenges and embracing resilience have been central to the success of *BMORENews.com*. By addressing financial, technological, content, and market challenges head-on, the platform has not only survived but thrived in the competitive digital media landscape. The lessons learned and strategies employed will continue to guide *BMORENews.com* as it moves forward, ensuring that it remains a vital and impactful voice in Black journalism. As *BMORENews.com* looks to the future, its commitment to innovation, integrity, and community will be the driving forces behind its continued success.

10

Chapter 10: The Future of Black Journalism

Introduction

The future of Black journalism is intertwined with the broader evolution of the media landscape. As digital technologies continue to reshape how news is produced and consumed, Black media outlets face unique opportunities and challenges. This chapter explores the future of Black journalism, highlighting the trends, innovations, and strategic initiatives that will shape the industry. It also reflects on the role of *BMORENews.com* in this evolving landscape and its commitment to fostering a vibrant, inclusive media environment.

Emerging Trends in Journalism

The media industry is undergoing rapid transformation, driven by technological advancements and changing audience behaviors. Several key trends are set to influence the future of Black journalism.

Digital-First Approach

As audiences increasingly consume news online, a digital-first approach has become essential. This shift involves prioritizing digital content production and distribution, leveraging social media platforms, and optimizing for mobile devices. Black media outlets must continue to embrace this approach to reach and engage their audiences effectively.

Data-Driven Journalism

Data-driven journalism uses data analytics to inform reporting and storytelling. By analyzing large datasets, journalists can uncover trends, patterns, and insights that enhance their reporting. Black media outlets can use data-driven journalism to highlight issues affecting Black communities, providing a nuanced and evidence-based perspective.

Multimedia Storytelling

Multimedia storytelling combines text, video, audio, and interactive elements to create engaging narratives. This approach allows for more dynamic and immersive content, catering to diverse audience preferences. Black media outlets can use multimedia storytelling to bring stories to life, capturing the richness and complexity of the Black experience.

The Role of Artificial Intelligence and Automation

Artificial Intelligence (AI) and automation are transforming journalism, offering new tools for content creation, distribution, and engagement.

AI in News Production

AI can assist in various aspects of news production, from generating news summaries to transcribing interviews. For Black media outlets, AI can streamline workflows, reduce costs, and increase efficiency, allowing journalists to focus on in-depth reporting and analysis.

Personalization and Audience Engagement

AI-powered algorithms can personalize content recommendations based on user preferences and behaviors. This personalization enhances audience engagement by delivering relevant and tailored content. Black media outlets can use AI to better understand their audiences and provide content that resonates with their unique interests and needs.

Various Software: "I am no techie!"
No matter your level of technical expertise, there's always a software solution that fits your needs. Running a website involves a continuous learning curve and the opportunity to tap into new, often untapped talent.

Here are some essential tools to consider:

- **Microsoft Publisher**: For desktop publishing.
- **Macromedia Dreamweaver & Fireworks**: Classic tools for web design and graphics.
- **Content Management Systems (CMS)**: For easy website management.
- **Magisto.com**: Perfect for beginners making videos.
- **Adobe Premier**: Ideal for more advanced video editing.
- **CapCut**: Free video editing software.

- **Canva**: For creating stunning graphics effortlessly.
- **Streamyard.com**: Stream video shows on Facebook, LinkedIn, Twitter, and YouTube.
- **Constant Contact & MailChimp**: For effective email marketing.
- **Fiverr**: A great platform to find affordable web designers and graphic artists.

There's a tool for everyone, regardless of how long it takes to find the right one.

The Importance of Community-Centric Journalism

Community-centric journalism prioritizes the needs and voices of the community it serves. For Black media outlets, this approach is critical to building trust, fostering engagement, and driving social change.

Hyperlocal Reporting

Hyperlocal reporting focuses on news and issues specific to a particular community or neighborhood. By covering local events, concerns, and achievements, Black media outlets can strengthen their connection with their audience and provide a platform for grassroots voices.

Advocacy and Social Impact

Black journalism has a long history of advocacy and social impact. Future Black media outlets must continue this tradition by championing social justice, highlighting systemic inequalities, and advocating for policy changes. This commitment to advocacy reinforces the role of Black media as a catalyst for positive change.

Strategic Initiatives for Black Media Sustainability

Sustainability is a pressing concern for many Black media outlets. Strategic initiatives can help ensure the long-term viability and impact of these organizations.

Diversifying Revenue Streams

To achieve financial stability, Black media outlets must diversify their revenue streams. In addition to traditional advertising, potential revenue sources include sponsored content, memberships, crowdfunding, events, and merchandise. Exploring these avenues can reduce reliance on a single revenue source and enhance financial resilience.

Building Strategic Partnerships

Forming strategic partnerships with other media organizations, nonprofits (like Fusion Partnership in Baltimore which assists organizations in getting their nonprofit self-sustaining), and community groups can provide valuable resources and support. These partnerships can enhance content quality, expand reach, and create opportunities for collaborative projects. Black media outlets can leverage these relationships to strengthen their impact and sustainability.

Investing in Talent and Training

Investing in talent development and training is essential for fostering innovation and maintaining high journalistic standards. Black media outlets should prioritize professional development opportunities for their staff, ensuring they have the skills and knowledge to navigate the evolving media landscape.

The Role of BMORENews.com in the Future of Black Journalism

As a digital-native platform, *BMORENews.com* is well-positioned to lead the charge in the future of Black journalism. Its commitment to innovation, community-centric reporting, and advocacy sets it apart as a model for other Black media outlets.

Embracing Technological Advancements

BMORENews.com will continue to embrace technological advancements, leveraging AI, data analytics, and multimedia storytelling to enhance its content and engagement. By staying at the forefront of digital innovation, *BMORENews.com* can provide timely, relevant, and impactful news to its audience.

Strengthening Community Engagement

Community engagement will remain a cornerstone of *BMORENews.com's* strategy. Through hyperlocal reporting, community forums, and events like the Joe Manns Black Wall Street Awards, the platform will continue to build strong connections with its audience and amplify grassroots voices.

Expanding Strategic Partnerships

BMORENews.com will seek to expand its strategic partnerships, collaborating with other media organizations, community groups, and advocacy organizations. These partnerships will enhance the platform's reach, resources, and impact, ensuring it remains a vital voice in Black journalism.

Conclusion

The future of Black journalism is filled with promise and potential. By embracing digital innovation, prioritizing community-centric reporting, and pursuing strategic initiatives, Black media outlets can navigate the challenges and opportunities of the evolving media landscape. *BMORENews.com*, with its commitment to excellence and community, will continue to play a pivotal role in shaping the future of Black journalism, ensuring that the voices of the Black community are heard, respected, and amplified. As we look ahead, the mission remains clear: to empower, inform, and inspire through the power of journalism.

11

Chapter 11: Comparative Analysis

Introduction

With the decline of print media, it's essential to examine the online presence of Black legacy newspapers and similar outlets, especially in the Baltimore-Washington D.C. corridor, which is home to over 2 million African Americans. This analysis aims to identify the strengths, weaknesses, opportunities, and threats (SWOT) of Black media to understand *BMORENews.com's* national standing. As of April 2024, this study focuses on Baltimore City (63% Black), Baltimore County (29% Black), Prince George's County (64% Black), and Washington D.C. (43% Black). Maryland's population is about 30% Black, translating into approximately 1.8 million people as of 2020, while D.C. has over 300,000 African Americans.

Prominent Newspapers in the Region

- *Afro-American Newspapers* **(est. 1892):** The oldest Black family newspaper in America has transitioned successfully to digital platforms.

- Strong online presence: Facebook (647k followers), Instagram (15k), Twitter (13.1k), YouTube (503 subscribers with 459 videos), TikTok (6,749 followers, 98.6k likes).
  - Includes online followers in distribution metrics while maintaining USPS distribution for print editions.
- **The Baltimore Times (est. 1986):**
  - Prints 14,000 newspapers weekly.
  - Social media presence: Facebook (4.2k followers), Twitter (2,527), Instagram (3,145).
- **Northwest Voice Newspaper (est. 2005):**
  - Distributes 8,000 newspapers monthly in northwest Baltimore County.
  - Online presence with 257 Facebook followers and a sizable email subscriber base of 6,000.
- **The Washington Informer:**
  - Circulates 16,000 newspapers weekly.
  - Robust social media: Facebook (9k followers), Twitter (12.7k), Instagram (10.4k), TikTok (290 followers, 400 likes), YouTube (821 subscribers, 920 videos).

BMORENews.com

- **Overview:** *BMORENews.com*, a digital-native platform with no print edition, has established a significant online audience.
  - Social media presence: Facebook (5.3k followers), TikTok (1.2k followers, 12.5k likes), Instagram (413 followers), YouTube (4k subscribers, 7k videos), Twitter (2,709 followers), LinkedIn (7,992 followers), and an email subscriber base over 1,300.

- Coverage includes local news in Baltimore and on-the-ground reports from the White House, Africa, the Middle East, the Caribbean, and Canada.
- Possesses one of the largest Black American news video libraries with over 7,000 videos.

Other Notable Black Newspapers

- *The Final Call Newspaper*:
  - Affiliated with the Nation of Islam, available in most cities with an NOI presence.
  - Strong online presence: Facebook (93,000+ followers), Instagram (29,000), Twitter (52,000+).
- *The Philadelphia Tribune*:
  - Reaches 625,000 readers weekly.
  - Significant social media presence: Facebook (25,000 followers), Instagram (6,889), YouTube (866), Twitter (23,800).
- *The Chicago Defender* (est. 1905):
  - Transitioned to a digitally-focused platform in July 2019.
  - Social media: Facebook (139,000 followers), Instagram (11,800), Twitter (8,693).
- *The New York Amsterdam News*:
  - Facebook (60,000 followers), Twitter (15,000+), Instagram (17,000+).
- *Atlanta Black Star (ABS)*:
  - Reaches over 5 million unique visitors per month.
  - Strong social media presence: Facebook (1.2 million followers), Twitter (42,000+), LinkedIn (657), YouTube (43,000 subscribers, 614 videos).

- *Black Enterprise Magazine:*
  - Strong online presence: Facebook (781,000 followers), Twitter (329,000+), LinkedIn (282,000+), Instagram (868,000+), YouTube (39,000 subscribers, 2,000 videos).

TikTok Followings

- *Afro-American Newspapers*: 98.7k likes, 6,732 followers.
- *Washington Informer*: 400 likes, 511 followers.
- *BMORENews*: 11.7k likes, 116 followers.
- *Chicago Defender*: 791 likes, 254 followers.
- *Atlanta Black Star*: 6,250 likes, 512 followers.
- *Black Enterprise*: 6,250 likes, 512 followers.

Noteworthy Sites

- *BlackNews.com*:
  - Created by Dante Lee, combines press releases with digital media.
  - Social media: Instagram (136k followers), Facebook (92.4k), Twitter (8,381).
- **Official Black Wall Street (OBWS):**
  - Owned by Mandy Bowman.
  - Social media: Instagram (990K followers), Facebook (144K), LinkedIn (80.5k), Twitter (17K), YouTube (2.7k subscribers, 29 videos), TikTok (1.6k followers, 13.3K likes).

Conclusion

By analyzing the digital footprint and competitive landscape of Black legacy newspapers and digital-native platforms in the Baltimore-Washington D.C. corridor and beyond, the analysis underscores the diverse strategies employed by these outlets to maintain relevance, engagement, and financial sustainability in an ever-evolving media environment. *BMORENews.com* stands out for its extensive video library, multi-regional coverage, and commitment to addressing issues pertinent to Black communities both locally and globally. This comprehensive digital strategy positions *BMORENews.com* as a leading voice in Black journalism.

12

Chapter 12: Reflections and Future Directions

Introduction

As we come to the end of this exploration of *BMORENews.com* and the digital revolution in Black journalism, it is essential to reflect on the journey, the lessons learned, and the future directions for the platform and the broader landscape of Black media. This chapter offers a comprehensive reflection on the key themes discussed in this book and outlines a vision for the future.

Reflections on the Journey

The Genesis of BMORENews.com

BMORENews.com was founded at a pivotal moment in the history of journalism, during the early days of the digital revolution. From its humble beginnings, the platform has grown into a significant voice in Black journalism, driven by a commitment to community empowerment, social justice, and innovation.

The Evolution of the Black Press

The Black Press has a rich history of advocacy, resilience, and impact. *BMORENews.com* is part of this legacy, carrying forward the tradition of amplifying Black voices and addressing issues that matter to the Black community. The platform's journey reflects the broader evolution of the Black Press in the digital age, navigating challenges and seizing opportunities to stay relevant and impactful.

Key Lessons Learned

The Power of Community-Centric Journalism

One of the most significant lessons from the *BMORENews.com* journey is the power of community-centric journalism. By prioritizing the needs and voices of the community, the platform has built trust, fostered engagement, and driven social change. This approach underscores the importance of staying connected to the community and serving as a platform for grassroots voices.

The Importance of Adaptation and Innovation

The media landscape is constantly evolving, and *BMORENews.com's* success has hinged on its ability to adapt and innovate. Embracing new technologies, exploring diverse revenue streams, and staying ahead of industry trends have been critical to maintaining relevance and sustainability. This lesson highlights the necessity of flexibility and continuous learning in the ever-changing world of journalism.

The Role of Strategic Partnerships

Strategic partnerships have been instrumental in *BMORE-News.com's* growth and impact. Collaborations with other media organizations, community groups, and advocacy organizations have provided valuable resources and support. These partnerships have enhanced the platform's reach, content quality, and influence, demonstrating the power of collective effort and shared goals.

Future Directions

Expanding Digital Innovation

Looking ahead, *BMORENews.com* will continue to expand its digital innovation efforts. This includes leveraging artificial intelligence, data analytics, and multimedia storytelling to enhance content production and audience engagement. By staying at the forefront of digital advancements, the platform can provide timely, relevant, and impactful news to its audience.

Deepening Community Engagement

Community engagement will remain a cornerstone of *BMORE-News.com's* strategy. The platform will continue to prioritize hyperlocal reporting, community forums, and events that foster connection and empowerment. By deepening its engagement with the community, *BMORENews.com* can ensure that it remains a vital and trusted source of information and advocacy.

Strengthening Financial Sustainability

Ensuring financial sustainability is crucial for the long-term success of *BMORENews.com*. The platform will continue to diversify its revenue streams, exploring opportunities such as memberships, crowdfunding, and strategic partnerships. By building a robust financial foundation, *BMORENews.com* can sustain its operations and continue to serve the community effectively.

Enhancing Talent Development

Investing in talent development is essential for fostering innovation and maintaining high journalistic standards. *BMORENews.com* will prioritize professional development opportunities for its team, ensuring they have the skills and knowledge to navigate the evolving media landscape. By cultivating a talented and motivated team, the platform can continue to produce high-quality and impactful journalism.

The Vision for the Future

A Leading Voice in Black Journalism

BMORENews.com aspires to be a leading voice in Black journalism, setting the standard for community-centric, innovative, and impactful reporting. By staying true to its mission and values, the platform can continue to amplify Black voices, address critical issues, and drive social change.

A Catalyst for Social Change

BMORENews.com aims to be a catalyst for social change, using journalism as a tool for advocacy and empowerment. By highlighting systemic inequalities, championing social justice, and advocating for policy changes, the platform can contribute to meaningful and lasting change in the Black community and beyond.

A Model for Digital Innovation

BMORENews.com envisions itself as a model for digital innovation in journalism. By embracing new technologies and exploring innovative approaches to content production and distribution, the platform can set an example for other media organizations. This commitment to innovation will ensure that *BMORENews.com* remains at the cutting edge of the industry.

Conclusion

The journey of *BMORENews.com* is a testament to the power of resilience, community, and innovation. As the platform looks to the future, it remains committed to its mission of empowering, informing, and inspiring through journalism. The lessons learned and the vision for the future outlined in this chapter will guide *BMORENews.com* as it continues to navigate the evolving media landscape. The platform's dedication to excellence, integrity, and community will ensure that it remains a vital and impactful voice in Black journalism for years to come.

13

Chapter 13: Celebrating Milestones and Looking Forward

Introduction

As *BMORENews.com* continues its journey, it is essential to celebrate the milestones achieved and set sights on the future. This chapter reflects on key accomplishments, acknowledges the support and partnerships that have been instrumental in the platform's success, and outlines future aspirations.

Celebrating Milestones

Founding and Growth

From its inception in 2002, *BMORENews.com* has grown from a small digital news platform to a significant voice in Black journalism. The platform has expanded its reach, diversified its content, and maintained a steadfast commitment to the community.

Coverage and Impact

BMORENews.com has covered critical issues affecting the Black community, from local news in Baltimore to international stories. The platform's comprehensive coverage has included on-the-ground reporting from the White House, Africa, the Middle East, the Caribbean, and Canada. With over 7,000 videos in its library, *BMORENews.com* boasts one of the largest collections of Black news video content.

Community Engagement

Through initiatives like the Joe Manns Black Wall Street Awards, political forums, and community meetings, *BMORENews.com* has fostered strong connections with its audience. These efforts have not only highlighted the achievements of Black entrepreneurs and professionals but have also provided a platform for important discussions and advocacy.

Acknowledging Support and Partnerships

Mentors and Advisors

The journey of *BMORENews.com* would not have been possible without the guidance and support of mentors and advisors. Individuals like Diane Bell McKoy, Michael Preston, Dr. Charles Simmons, and J. Howard Henderson have provided invaluable advice and encouragement. Their mentorship has been a cornerstone of the platform's growth and success.

Strategic Partnerships

Strategic partnerships have played a crucial role in enhancing *BMORENews.com's* reach and impact. Collaborations with other media organizations, community groups, and advocacy organizations have provided valuable resources and support. These partnerships have enabled the platform to expand its content, engage new audiences, and drive social change.

Community Support

The unwavering support of the community has been instrumental in *BMORENews.com's* success. From readers and viewers to advertisers and sponsors, the community's trust and engagement have fueled the platform's growth. *BMORENews.com* is deeply grateful for this support and remains committed to serving the community.

Future Aspirations

Enhancing Digital Capabilities

As technology continues to evolve, *BMORENews.com* will focus on enhancing its digital capabilities. This includes leveraging artificial intelligence, data analytics, and multimedia storytelling to improve content production and audience engagement. The platform aims to stay at the forefront of digital innovation, providing timely, relevant, and impactful news.

Expanding Reach and Influence

BMORENews.com aspires to expand its reach and influence, both locally and globally. By increasing its presence on social media, exploring new distribution channels, and forming new strategic partnerships, the platform aims to reach a broader audience and amplify its impact.

Fostering Next-Generation Journalists

Investing in the next generation of journalists is a priority for *BMORENews.com*. The platform will provide professional development opportunities, mentorship, and training programs to nurture emerging talent. By fostering a new generation of journalists, *BMORENews.com* aims to ensure the sustainability and growth of Black journalism.

Advocating for Social Justice

Advocacy for social justice will remain a core focus of *BMORENews.com*. The platform will continue to highlight systemic inequalities, champion social justice causes, and advocate for policy changes. By using journalism as a tool for advocacy, *BMORENews.com* aims to drive meaningful and lasting change.

Conclusion

As *BMORENews.com* reflects on its journey and celebrates its milestones, it looks forward to the future with optimism and determination. The platform's commitment to innovation, community, and advocacy will guide its path forward. By staying true to its mission and values, *BMORENews.com* will continue to empower, inform, and inspire, ensuring that the voices of the Black community are heard, respected, and amplified. The future is bright, and *BMORENews.com* is ready to embrace the opportunities and challenges that lie ahead.

JOURNAPRENEUR: Pioneering the Digital Age of Black Journalism encapsulates the remarkable journey of a pioneering digital news platform that has not only survived but thrived amidst the seismic shifts in the journalism landscape. Founded in 2002, *BMORENews.com* has grown from a fledgling digital outlet into an anchor of the Black Press, offering a powerful voice for the African American community and serving as a beacon of innovation, resilience, and advocacy.

The journey of *BMORENews.com* reflects the broader evolution of the Black Press, which has always been more than just a medium for news dissemination. It has been a platform for social justice, a catalyst for community engagement, and a crucial tool for empowerment. As the digital age transforms how we consume and interact with news, *BMORENews.com* has adeptly navigated these changes, leveraging technology to enhance its reach and impact.

Central to *BMORENews.com's* success is its unwavering commitment to community-centric journalism. By prioritizing the needs and voices of the community, the platform has built trust and fostered strong connections. Initiatives like the Joe Manns Black Wall Street Awards and various community forums have highlighted the achievements of Black entrepreneurs and professionals, creating a sense of pride and solidarity.

The support and mentorship from visionary leaders have been instrumental in guiding *BMORENews.com*. The strategic partnerships forged with other media organizations, community groups, and advocacy organizations have provided valuable resources and broadened the platform's influence. These collaborations have reinforced the belief that working together can achieve greater impact than operating in isolation.

As *BMORENews.com* looks to the future, it does so with optimism and a clear vision. Enhancing digital capabilities, expanding reach, fostering the next generation of journalists, and advocating for social justice will remain at the forefront of its mission. The platform's adaptability and commitment to innovation ensure that it will continue to evolve and meet the needs of its audience in a rapidly changing media landscape.

The story of *BMORENews.com* is a testament to the power of resilience, community, and innovation. It demonstrates that with a clear vision, unwavering commitment, and a willingness to adapt, it is possible to overcome challenges and make a lasting impact. As we celebrate the milestones achieved and look forward to future aspirations, *BMORENews.com* stands as a shining example of the transformative power of journalism in the digital age.

In conclusion, *BMORENews.com* is more than just a digital news platform; it is a movement that empowers, informs, and inspires. It is a testament to the enduring legacy of the Black Press and a beacon of hope for future generations. By staying true to its mission and values, *BMORENews.com* will continue to be a vital and impactful voice, ensuring that the stories and voices of the Black community are heard, respected, and amplified. The future is bright, and *BMORENews.com* is ready to embrace the opportunities and challenges that lie ahead, continuing to make a difference, one story at a time.

EPILOGUE

The truth is, a true journapreneur can be intimidating to many. People never know what I'm going to say or what's coming next. They never know which hat I'm wearing – the entrepreneur or the journalist. They wonder if I'm talking business deals or political economy, the intersection of business and politics, like our politicians and their ability to bring home the bacon. Am I the Doni discussing civil rights issues, like Freddie Gray, or the Doni highlighting how America, with just 5% of the world's population, houses 25% of the world's incarcerated persons, 35% of whom are Black men like me and Black women the fastest growing demographic?

When I call, the first thing people try to figure out is which Doni they're dealing with – the one looking to do business or the one chasing the breaking story. It can be challenging to navigate these dual roles, always keeping your head on a swivel from a professional perspective. I strive to present myself as controlled and mild-mannered, but sometimes I get passionate about issues, and that's okay. It's okay to feel that way. I have to remind myself constantly that it's okay to be human and to get passionate about certain topics.

As I regularly ride past Pimlico Racetrack, I often question what has happened to the Racetrack Impact funds promised to Park Heights through various pieces of legislation. While the white communities to the north and northeast seem to benefit, the predominantly Black neighborhoods to the west and south of Pimlico

EPILOGUE

Racetrack in northwest Baltimore face constant excuses and delays. Baltimore's long history of segregation, dating back to Mayor J. Barry Mahool in 1910, still casts a shadow today. Notably, two Black attorneys, George McMechen and Ashbie Hawkins, were relentless in challenging Mahool's segregationist policies.

There's much to be unearthed, unmasked, and addressed to ensure that this 63% Black and 73% Black and brown city can better serve all its citizens. I've been following the Park Heights and Pimlico story for 20 years, questioning whether Park Heights below Northern Parkway will receive the same benefits as the non-Black communities above it. This dual role often requires me to switch hats – sometimes I report the story, and other times I speak on behalf of the city where I have spent 57 of my 59 years.

From South Baltimore's Sharp Leadenhall, where figures like Joseph H. Brown and Alice Torriente got their start, to East Baltimore, home to Reginald F. Lewis, William C. March Funeral Home, and the Isaac Myers/Frederick Douglass Maritime Park and Museum – where Myers helped start the national Black labor union movement – to West Baltimore, home to the Mitchell Family, Little Willie Adams, and Tom Smith (a significant figure before Little Willie), I specialize in covering this city and love doing business here. I also cover northwest Baltimore County where the clear majority is Black, gorgeous Prince George's County (once hailed as the wealthiest Black jurisdiction in the state), and Washington, D.C. – which is no longer majority Black.

I have immense respect for the Black-owned business owners and entrepreneurs in my hometown who, every single day, go out and give it their all. Entrepreneurs are some of the boldest people in the world; they understand that if they don't hustle, they don't eat. They could choose to stay home, but instead, they hustle from dawn until dusk to produce, serve, and build. This city instilled that

EPILOGUE

spirit in me from the time I sold Afro newspapers on the largest route in West Baltimore. My parents taught me to get out there and make things happen. When your house, marriage, and relationships are on the line, it means you are all in, ten toes down, completely committed.

As the son of two entrepreneurs and the proud father of at least one – my 23-year-old daughter, N'yinde, who has run a beauty product business since she was 16 – I take great pride in the roles I play. I have strived to listen to my inner voice and do what I believe God put me here to do. One of my greatest joys is mentoring the next generation of journapreneurs: those with the courage to do what I do but even better. Outshine me, surpass my accomplishments, break my records. But as you do, make sure to pass the baton to those who come after you.

This book explores the intersection of journalism and business in the post-digital era, with a particular focus on my deep appreciation for Black-owned businesses. The Joe Manns Black Wall Street Awards are just one expression of this passion. Growing up, I was acutely aware that our communities thrive when Black-owned businesses flourish. In my upbringing, the banker, barber, beautician, insurance agent, home contractor, and mechanic were all Black. My parents never explicitly mentioned "Black Wall Street," but they embodied its principles in every way. Whether they knew about it or not, they lived it.

My dad educated me about the North Carolina Mutual Life Insurance Company in Durham, one of the three recognized Black Wall Streets. He also taught me about his national association of Black funeral directors that met annually. My mom showed me how to hustle by selling her chicken sandwiches at Easterwood Park flag football games every Sunday and helped me manage the money I earned selling *Afro* newspapers each week. I am grateful for how

EPILOGUE

they nurtured my awareness of the Black business owners in our community, from mechanic shops and cleaners to oil companies, accounting firms, construction firms, and stores. This foundation shaped my understanding of the critical role these businesses play in empowering our communities.

Growing up that way instilled in me a strong work ethic from a young age, and I thank God for that upbringing. It has shaped me into who I am today. As a community, we have $1.6 trillion in annual disposable income – roughly the 16th largest economy on earth. I want to see this economic power help grow our businesses and, in turn, empower our communities. Former Maryland Lt. Gov. Boyd Rutherford often said, "No one is going to hire Black people more than Black people." This is especially important when it comes to hiring our brothers and sisters who have just served time. If anyone understands their struggles, it's us. If anyone is going to help them, it better be us.

On that note, I want to extend a very special word of gratitude to those beyond Baltimore who have helped me and my business expand its territory. These individuals include Lee Vaughn (MD), Walter Edwards (NY), Regina Smith (NY), Monique Hector (NY), Asha Roper (NY), Bou Kahn (NY/GA), Robert Scott (GA), Morocco Coleman (GA), Dr. Wilbert Wilson (MD), Corey "Bing" Mathis (LA), and Beverly Smith (DC). Thanks also goes to Bishop Kevia F. Elliott (MD), Avon Bellamy (MD), Jacqueline Cummings (MD), Micheline Bowman (MD/DC), Cynthia Boykin (IL), Pam Perry (MI), Rodney Burris (MD), Marc Clarke (MD/DC), Marsha Jews (MD), Michael Haynie (MD/FL/Kenya), Frank Johnson (MD), Marsha Jews (MD), Meshelle Howard (MD/DC), Ricky Smith (MD/DC), Mark Spencer (MD/DC), Diane Bell-McKoy, Calvin Watkins (MD), Kenny Brown (MD), Jake Oliver (MD),

EPILOGUE

Harold Hayley (MD), Dr. Michael Carter (CA), and Douglass "Art" Blacksher (CA).

To the Historically Black Colleges and Universities that birthed and nurtured my academic pursuits – Morehouse College, Coppin State University (Ronald E. McNair Post-Baccalaureate Achievement Program Scholar), and Morgan State University - I know I stand on the shoulders of giants and am here to serve people, beginning in my very own neighborhood – which happens to be my beloved Sandtown Community in Historic West Baltimore!

Dr. Tyrone Taborn (STEMCITYUSA.com by Career Communications Group), Rondy Griffin, Vennieth McCormick (New Life Recovery Network): You guys are the best! Tony Randall of Next Phaze Café, my Salvation Army of Central Maryland Family – including the man who drafted me to help, John Davis, Mike Posko of Chesapeake Habitat for Humanity, Attorney Extraordinare William "Billy" Murphy, Esquire and his firm - Murphy, Falcon, & Murphy, Terence Dickson of Terra Café Bmore, Renny Bass, Tony Randall of Next Phaze Café, Robert Dashiell, Esquire, Kevin Johnson and Commercial Construction, Marty Glaze, Zachary McDaniels, and caterer Jimmy Britton who said to me many years ago, "The slickest thing a person can ever do is stop being slick."

Pamela Reaves, Deborah Hardnett, Dr. Leroy McKenzie, Robert Ingram, Richard D. Elliott, Nicole Kirby, Kermit "K.C." Carter, Hassan Giordano, Andy Pierre, Clarence "Tiger" Davis, Kevin Peck (Poly and Morehouse schoolmate) and the *Afro American Newspapers* Family, Jake Oliver – former Publisher of the *Afro American Newspapers*, Congressman Kweisi Mfume and the WEAA Family including Mike Nyce, my beautiful *Baltimore Times* Family, Ron Burke and the *Washington Informer* Family, and the incomparable Charles Robinson of MPT.

EPILOGUE

Thank you to Larry Gaines, Mo Tilghman, and the Bailbondsmen of Baltimore. Thank you to Leon Purnell and the Men's Center in Historic East Baltimore.

Thank you to Tonya Denise Jeffries for your advice, insight, and wisdom. I bounced a lot off of you and you not once complained. And a very special thank you to Bishop Barry Chapman for believing in me and my business.

And to any and every person who ever helped me along this journey, please forgive my omission of your name. In deepest gratitude, I promise you I strive every single day to pay it forward.

Therefore, at this juncture in my 30-year career as a journalist and a lifetime as an entrepreneur, the most important thing for me is encouraging the next generation. Passing the ball is what matters most to me.

In conclusion, being a certified journapreneur means navigating the delicate balance between journalism and entrepreneurship, often wearing multiple hats and tackling diverse issues. It's a path that can be challenging and intimidating, but it is also deeply rewarding. From questioning the distribution of Pimlico Racetrack funds to championing civil rights and economic empowerment, my journey has been about more than just reporting stories—it's been about making a tangible difference in my community. I have immense respect for the Black-owned business owners and entrepreneurs who hustle daily to build, serve, and inspire. This book celebrates that spirit and underscores the importance of using our collective economic power to uplift our communities. As I look back on my 30-year career, my greatest joy comes from mentoring the next generation of journapreneurs. I encourage them to surpass my accomplishments and continue the legacy of passing the ball forward. Let us all strive to outshine, outdo, and uplift, ensuring that we leave a lasting impact for those who follow.

AFTERWORD

What an esteemed honor to write the afterword for this historic book. I am grateful for the opportunity.

As we reach the conclusion of "JOURNAPRENEUR: Pioneering the Digital Age of Black Journalism," it is essential to reflect on the journey, the lessons learned, and the road ahead. This book is more than a chronicle of *BMORENews.com*; it is a testament to the resilience, innovation, and unwavering commitment to the principles of Black journalism.

Reflecting on the Journey

From its inception in 2002, *BMORENews.com* was born out of a necessity to amplify Black voices and cover stories that mainstream media often overlooked. Through perseverance, strategic innovation, and a deep connection to the community, *BMORENews.com* has grown into a formidable force in digital journalism. This journey was marked by significant milestones, including the creation of one of the largest Black news video libraries and the establishment of the Joe Manns Black Wall Street Awards, honoring over 2700 individuals across major U.S. cities.

Lessons Learned

AFTERWORD

1. **The Power of Community-Centric Journalism**: Our commitment to prioritizing the needs and voices of the community has built trust and fostered strong connections. This approach has been crucial in driving social change and community empowerment.
2. **The Importance of Adaptation and Innovation**: Embracing digital tools and staying ahead of industry trends have been vital in maintaining relevance and sustainability. Continuous learning and flexibility have been key to navigating the ever-changing media landscape.
3. **The Role of Strategic Partnerships**: Collaborations with other media organizations, community groups, and advocacy organizations have provided valuable resources and support, enhancing our reach and impact.

Future Directions

Looking ahead, *BMORENews.com* will continue to expand its digital innovation efforts, deepen community engagement, and ensure financial sustainability. Investing in talent development and fostering the next generation of journalists will remain a priority. Advocacy for social justice will continue to be at the forefront of our mission, using journalism as a tool for meaningful and lasting change.

A Vision for the Future

BMORENews.com aspires to be a leading voice in Black journalism, setting the standard for community-centric, innovative, and impactful reporting. We envision ourselves as a catalyst for social change and a model for digital innovation in journalism. By staying true to our mission and values, we will continue to amplify Black voices, address critical issues, and drive social change.

Conclusion

The story of *BMORENews.com* is a testament to the power of resilience, community, and innovation. As we look to the future, we remain committed to our mission of empowering, informing, and inspiring through journalism. The lessons learned and the vision for the future outlined in this book will guide us as we navigate the evolving media landscape. By staying true to our mission and values, *BMORENews.com* will continue to be a vital and impactful voice, ensuring that the stories and voices of the Black community are heard, respected, and amplified.

Super Congratulations, Doni Glover, on your third book. This by far is another home run.

Deborah Hardnett | CEO, Wealthy Sistas Media Group

19

Joe Manns
Black Wall Street
Awards
Harlem

20

Joe Manns
Black Wall Street
Awards
Southeast
DC

21

Joe Manns
Black Wall Street
Awards
Brooklyn at
Weeksville
Heritage Center

22

Joe Manns
Black Wall Street
Awards
Prince Georges
County, MD

23

Joe Manns
Black Wall Street
Awards
Richmond, VA

24

Joe Manns
Black Wall Street
Awards
Brooklyn at
Borough Hall

25

Joe Manns
Black Wall Street
Awards
New Orleans

26

Joe Manns
Black Wall Street
Awards
Featuring
Entrepreneur
Lance London,
proprietor of
Carolina Kitchen
Bar & Grill

27

Joe Manns
Black Wall Street
Awards
Baltimore

28

Joe Manns
Black Wall Street
Awards
Atlanta

29

Joe Manns
Black Wall Street
Awards
Howard
University

30

Joe Manns
Black Wall Street
Awards
Bowie

31

Doni on one of his numerous White House Visits.

32

BMORENews.com
The News
Before the News

33

Montego Bay, Jamaica
Sam Sharpe Square

PHOTO GALLERY LISTING

1. Doni and The Honorable Governor of Maryland, Wes Moore.

2. Doni on WBAL TV11, Political Analyst.

3. Doni on Fox 5, Freddie Gray Interview.

4. Doni with Press Secretary Karine Jeanne-Pierre.

5. Doni with Sunny Hostin, CNN.

6. Doni with Susan Rice, an American diplomat, policy advisor, and public official. As a member of the Democratic Party, Rice served as the 22nd Director of the United States Domestic Policy Council from 2021 to 2023, as the 27th U.S. Ambassador to the United Nations from 2009 to 2013, and as the 23rd U.S. National Security Advisor from 2013 to 2017.

7. Doni hosted his own show on Radio One Baltimore's WOLB 1010 AM. It was the longest-running sponsored show on all of Radio One in the United States for 21 years. Doni left and started his own streaming network with the help of Michael Haynie, BlackUSA.News.

PHOTO GALLERY LISTING

8. Doni in Jordan.

9. Washington, D.C. "Mayor for Life" Marion Barry was spectacular for Black business development in the DMV (DC, Maryland, Virginia).

10. BET's Ed Gordon and Doni at White House Juneteenth Celebration 2024.

11. 1st Lady of Maryland Yumi Hogan, Doni, and his "adopted mom," Diane Bell-McKoy. Circa 2015.

12. Doni in Tanzania.

13. Doni on CNN, Freddie Gray Interview.

14. Doni meets former San Francisco Mayor and former California General Assembly Speaker Willie Brown in Portland at National Newspaper Publishers Association Convention, 2014.

15. Attorney Billy Murphy has advertised his law firm - Murphy, Falcon, and Murphy - on BMORENews.com for nearly 20 years.

16. Doni in Ethiopia.

17. Doni Glover and "Bo" Obama, White House. Circa 2009.

18. Doni's was a regular on WBAL TV11 as a Political Analyst.

19. – 33. Listed on Gallery Pages

34. With NNPA's Stacy Brown and NNPA Pres. & CEO Ben Chavis at Baltimore Convention, 2024.

35. NNPA Convention, Baltimore, 2024.

36. With Kevin and Dana Peck of the Baltimore Afro-American at NNPA Convention in Baltimore, 2024. Kevin is Doni's Morehouse and Baltimore Polytechnic Institute schoolmate.

37. Cheryl Smith, the publisher of I Messenger News Group, which includes Texas Metro News, Garland Journal and I Messenger. Photo taken at NNPA Convention in Baltimore, 2024.

38. Robert W. Bogle president and CEO of The Philadelphia Tribune newspaper, where he has worked for 39 years. Bogle joined The Philadelphia Tribune in 1970 selling advertising. Bogle has been a community leader for many years and is especially active in the advancements of black Philadelphians. Photo taken at NNPA Convention in Baltimore, 2024.

REFERENCES

Abernathy, P. M. (n.d.). Saving community journalism: The path to profitability - JSTOR. JSTOR. Retrieved April 21, 2023, from https://www.jstor.org/stable/10.5149/9781469615431_abernathy

Adam, J. W. (2008). Innovation Management and U.S. Weekly Newspaper Web Sites: An Examination of newspaper managers and Emerging Technology. Taylor & Francis. Retrieved April 20, 2023, from https://www.tandfonline.com/doi/full/10.1080/14241270802000454

Black Media Initiative, https://www.journalism.cuny.edu/centers/center-community-media/black-media-initiative/

Chicago Defender Media Kit, 2021.

Detweiler, Frederick German. *The Negro Press in the United States*. University of Chicago. 1922.

Ellison, Ralph. *Invisible Man*.

Fanon, Frantz. *Wretched of the Earth*.

Faustino, Paulo. (2023), *'Business models and sustainability in the newspaper industry: Perspectives from European and North American executives.'* Journal of Digital Media & Policy, 14

REFERENCES

: 1, pp. 47–66. https://doi-org.proxy-ms.researchport.umd.edu/10.1386/jdmp_00097_1

Freire, Paulo. *Pedagogy of the Oppressed.*

Govenden, P. (2022, August). Does Black Economic Empowerment ownership matter? A decolonial analysis of "black visibility" in South Africa's print media content, 1994–2014. Taylor & Francis. Retrieved April 20, 2023, from https://www.tandfonline.com/doi/full/10.1080/23743670.2022.2096090

Han, X., & Lin, F. (2021, June 8). *Perceptions of the media's role and job satisfaction: A survey of journalists in Xinjiang.* Taylor & Francis. Retrieved April 20, 2023, from https://www.tandfonline.com/doi/full/10.1080/01292986.2021.1937247

Hilliard, Asa. *The Maroon Within Us.*

Horne, Gerald (2017). *The Rise & Fall of the Associated Negro Press – Claude Barnett's Pan-African News and the Jim Crow Paradox.* University of Illinois Press. p. 153. ISBN 9780252099762.

Hovenkamp, Herbert. *Antitrust and Platform Monopoly.* Yale Law Journal. Jun2021, Vol. 130 Issue 8, p1952-2050. 99p.

James, Winston. *The Struggles of John Brown Russwurm: The Life and Writings of a Pan-Africanist Pioneer, 1799-1851.* New York University Press. Kingston.

Karimi, Jahangir, Walter, Zhiping, *The Role of Dynamic Capabilities in Responding to Digital Disruption: A Factor-Based Study of the Newspaper Industry.* Journal of Management Information Systems, 07421222, Summer2015, Vol. 32, Issue 1.

REFERENCES

Lewis, Seth C.; Mass Communication & Society, Vol 15(3), May, 2012 pp. 309-334. Publisher: Taylor & Francis. DOI: 10.1080/15205436.2011.611607.

Lim, Joon Soo, Shin, Donghee, Zhang, Jun, Masiclat, Stephen, Luttrell, Regina, Kinsey, Dennis, Audiences in the Age of Artificial Intelligence: Perceptions and Behaviors of Optimizers, Mainstreamers, and Skeptics. Journal of Broadcasting & Electronic Media, 08838151, Jul2023, Vol. 67, Issue 3 News.

Media, C. for C. (2022, January 12). Mapping black media. Newmark J-School. Retrieved April 20, 2023, from https://www.journalism.cuny.edu/2020/11/mapping-black-media/

Naisbitt, John, Megatrends 2000. 1991.

Pew Research Center, Circulation of paid black-oriented newspapers, July 27, 2021. https://www.pewresearch.org/journalism/chart/sotnm-hispanic-black-african-american-newspaper-circulation/

Philadelphia Tribune Media Kit, 2024.

Retis, J., & Chacon, L. (n.d.). *Mapping digital-native U.S. Latinx News: Beyond geographical boundaries, language barriers, and hyper-fragmentation of audiences.* International Symposium on Online Journalism. Retrieved April 20, 2023, from https://isoj.org/research/mapping-digital-native-u-s-latinx-news-beyond-geographical-boundaries-language-barriers-and-hyper-fragmentation-of-audiences/

Rogers, E. M. 2003. *Diffusion of innovations.* 5th ed. New York: Free Press.

REFERENCES

Ross, Felicia Jones. *Black Press Scholarship: Where We Have Been, Where We Are, and Where We Need to Go.* American Journalism. Summer 2020, Vol. 37 Issue 3, p301-320. 20p. DOI: 10.1080/08821127.2020.1790846.

Ruotsalainen, Juho; Heinonen, Sirkka; Hujanen, Jaana; Villi, Mikko. Pioneers as Peers: How Entrepreneurial Journalists Imagine the Futures of Journalism. Digital Journalism, July 2023, Vol. 11 Issue: 6 p1045-1064, 20p.

Shearer, E., Forman-Katz, N., & Khuzam, M. (2023, January 9). Hispanic and Black News Media Fact sheet. Pew Research Center's Journalism Project. Retrieved April 20, 2023, from https://www.pewresearch.org/journalism/fact-sheet/hispanic-and-black-news-media/

Singer, Jane. Innovation and Entrepreneurship: Journalism Students' Interpretive Repertoires for a Changing Occupation. Published online: 08 Apr 2019. https://doi.org/10.1080/17512786.2019.1602478

"The Best Kept Secret in American Journalism: The Associated Negro Press". Njhumanities.org. 4 October 2017. Retrieved 27 March 2024.

Reference: Walker, Maleo. Honoring African American Contributions: The Newspapers. Library of Congress. July 30, 2020. https://blogs.loc.gov/headlinesandheroes/2020/07/honoring-african-american-contributions-the-newspapers/

Williams, Fayne, *The Great Digital Migration: Exploring What Constitutes the Black Press Online.* Journalism & Mass Communication Quarterly, 10776990, Autumn2020, Vol. 97, Issue 3.

ABOUT THE AUTHOR

Born on June 27, 1965, in Baltimore's Provident Hospital to Lillie and Donald Edward Glover, Donald Morton "Doni" Glover is the CEO of DMGlobal – a multimedia marketing and public relations firm he founded in 2002 that services businesses, politicians, lawyers, nonprofits, corporations, municipalities, artists, and authors. He has covered news locally and nationally, including over 50 visits to the White House, and on-the-ground coverage in Jordan (2002) as US troops were landing to invade Iraq, the Ethiopian elections (2006), Tanzania, Jamaica, and Canada. He has been featured on NBC's WBAL TV-11, CNN, TV One, Fox News, Maryland Public Television, Spanish TV, WEAA, WYPR, Radio 103.9 New York, and in McClatchy Newspapers, the Final Call, the Afro-American Newspaper, the Washington Post, the Baltimore Sun, the Baltimore Brew, the Baltimore Business Journal, the Northwest Voice Newspaper, and the Baltimore Banner.

The 29-year veteran journalist is also the publisher of their flagship established in 2002, *BMORENews.com*, and BlackUSA.News (Est. 2020), and he's the host and producer of the Emmy-nominated weekday morning news platform – Doni Glover Show.

Further, he is the News Director for STEMCityUSA.com, founded by Dr. Tyrone Taborn's visionary contribution to ensure that Black

ABOUT THE AUTHOR

and brown people have a safe place in the Metaverse.

Glover launched DMGlobal after his stint concluded at Empower Baltimore Management Corporation (EBMC), the $100 million dollar federally-funded Empowerment Zone charged with helping transform parts of East and West Baltimore. There, he served for three years as a public information specialist. Prior to that, Glover was Editor of the Sandtown-Winchester VIEWPOINT Newspaper, a community-oriented publication that reached the 72 square blocks of this Historic West Baltimore community, from 1994 to 2000.

A Ronald E. McNair Honors graduate from Coppin State University with a Bachelor's degree in English: Media Arts: Broadcast Production and Technology, Glover actually began his academic career at Morehouse College. At present, he is working to complete his Master's in Journalism at the National Treasure, Morgan State University, in December 2024. His ultimate academic goal is to obtain a doctorate.

For the past twenty-two years as a journapreneur, the award-winning journalist's star in the world of media has certainly risen. With over 20 years of news talk hosting under his belt at Radio One Baltimore's WOLB 1010 AM, Glover has since taken his Doni Glover Show to the web Monday thru Friday at 9 am EST via YouTube, LinkedIn, Twitter, and Facebook. Speaking of which, Glover has clearly demonstrated how social media can propel one's reach to as many as 200,000 followers on social media.

Glover has used his platforms, including his flagship, www.bmorenews.com, to highlight and bring attention to the developments in the Black community as they unfold. While *BMORENews'* primary

ABOUT THE AUTHOR

news beat is Baltimore City, it also covers major Black enclaves, including northwest Baltimore County, Howard County, Prince George's County, the Eastern Shore of Maryland, and Washington, D.C. Further, Glover has covered news across the country, including three about four dozen visits to the White House.

BMORENews' agenda has always been the same: Black business, public education, returning citizens' services, affordable housing, and universal access to healthcare. With that in mind, almost every major politician in the state has been featured on *BMORENews*, which boasts a YouTube library of over 7,000 original clips.

Since the onset of *BMORENews*, Glover has hosted business networking events across the region. What started off as the Harambee Dinner Club eventually morphed into the Joe Manns Black Wall Street Awards, designed to celebrate Black entrepreneurs and professionals as well as the people who support them regardless of race. To date, over 2,500 individuals have been recognized in 9 major US cities: New York, Baltimore, Washington D.C., Richmond, Atlanta, New Orleans, Montgomery, Las Vegas, Tulsa, and Detroit. Furthermore, Glover has hosted two Annual National Black Wall Street Summits (2018 & 2019).

It should also be noted that Glover has been active in Maryland politics since 1998. Further, he has advised a number of winning political candidates on the local, state, and federal levels.

The author of "Unapologetically Black: Doni Glover Autobiography" (2015), Glover published his second book, "I Am Black Wall Street", in June 2021. This new book covers the history behind Tulsa's Black Wall Street from a national perspective.

ABOUT THE AUTHOR

Further, Glover launched BlackUSA.News as his pandemic pivot on December 1, 2020, and is now broadcasting 7 days a week on Facebook, LinkedIn, Twitter, and YouTube. The network features a number of hosts from around the country, including Doug Blacksher, Dr. Ashley Coleman, Dave Loveless, Quida Chancey, Dr. Ashley Coleman, Tasemere Gathers, Yolanda Pulley, Donna Tabron, Jason Rodriguez, and Ericka Alston Buck.

"I would say my biggest passion is helping the plight of America's Black-owned businesses. Nationally, we have approximately $1.6 trillion in annual disposable income. To me, that says that regardless of what political party is in power, we have enough resources to fix any problems we might have. And that's exactly why telling the world about our Black Wall Street history nationally is so important to me. If our ancestors were able to survive lynching, murder, rape, and terror and still build successful Black business communities, then we literally have no excuse today – no matter what we think. Otherwise, we are like beggars sitting on bags of gold!"

He continued, "Additionally, the Black Press must keep the spotlight on mass incarceration in America. And this it is so important to properly fund and support our public schools. While the US is only 5% of the world's population, we have 25% of the world's incarcerated persons. 35% of them look like me, Black and male while Black women are the fastest growing demographic amidst a prison industrial complex that is steeped in greed and profit. Clearly, we must reverse this burgeoning trend where we now have two and three generations from the same family in the same prison. Something is fundamentally wrong when 15% of the US population is occupying nearly 40% of the prisons."

ABOUT THE AUTHOR

You can also catch Glover on Thursdays at midnight on "Hiphop Chronicles" with Mike Nyce on Morgan State University's WEAA 88.9 FM. Each week, he gives the *BMORENews* Report on developments in the community, including updates on City Hall and Annapolis. Glover first appeared on WEAA (and also WEBB) in 1980 at the age of 15 with community leader Charlie Dugger. He has also hosted his own show for a time there called 'One Mic'.

Glover said he strives to live by his father's motto: "With a closed hand, nothing gets in and nothing gets out. With an open hand, there are endless possibilities. The moral of the story is 'Help somebody'!"

On that note, Glover is active in his own beloved Sandtown community in Historic West Baltimore and works with a number of organizations each year that are making a difference, including James Mosher Baseball, Black Professional Men, the Men's Center of East Baltimore, the Bea Gaddy Center, Upton Boxing, Choo Smith Youth Empowerment, Gregory Branch's Annual Legends Tournament at the Dome, the Salvation Army of Central Maryland (Board member), and the Annual Historic Pennsylvania Avenue Parade.

Glover's father was Donald Edward Glover. His mother was Lillie Juanita James Glover. The family-owned Glover's Funeral Home in the 60s, 70s, and 80s, first at Patterson Park and Lanvale, then 712-714 E. North Avenue, and lastly at 802 Madison Avenue up unto the mid-80s. It was there that the entrepreneurial bug was birthed in him. While his parents are both deceased, Glover is the very proud father of one son, Asaan Payton Glover, and one daughter, N'yinde' Amaari Glover. He is also a grandfather to Amari

ABOUT THE AUTHOR

(grandson), Satori (granddaughter), and the latest – Avani (granddaughter). And his beloved German Shepherd is named Pharaoh.